Sexpectations Girl provides honest and straightforward information that will help you make your own healthy choices. *Sexpectations* talks to girls (and guys) about when to have sex, how sex happens, why you might (or might not) have sex, what does sex feel like and other important things to know if and when a girl has, or is about to have, sex.

But sex isn't just about one person. *Sexpectations* also discusses what's happening with relationships and friends, family, sexual identity and cultural influences. Knowing about and making decisions about sex can be confusing at the best of times. This book will take you through knowing yourself and your body, keeping safe, protecting yourself, thinking through pregnancy, knowing about relationships and tapping into your personal power to make positive choices.

With comments from other girls facing the same experience, *Sexpectations* talks honestly and respectfully about the hard questions and gives you some answers you might need.

SEXPECTATIONS GIRL

LEISSA PITTS

CONTENTS

About Me

So why am I writing for girls about sex?

Sex is one of the most natural things in the world. It is also one of the most powerful and interesting things to talk and to know about. Sex is a big part of you evolving gradually and growing through your body, emotions and your social world into an adult. These kinds of changes can be difficult to understand because they happen without much of a guide book.

A little knowledge can go a long way for all young people, and understanding the reality of sex can give you opportunities to choose. I believe passionately in the right of young people to have the best information they can get to make the most important and considered decisions for themselves. No matter where young people come from or their life experience, education or culture, they have the right to access information from a balanced and non-judgemental perspective in order to create the best, most fulfilling life possible. And knowing about sex and relationships is one of the most important 'tool kits' you will ever acquire, finetune and use for your whole life.

Professionally, I've been a family and adolescent worker, counsellor, educator and sexual health promotion worker for young people and their families. I've worked with vulnerable and at-risk young people and families. I've managed programs in Australia and in other countries to improve access for women, men and young people to sexual health services and information. I've also completed a Masters degree in this area, which has been a door to many opportunities.

I've been talking about sex and relationships for many years with people from all walks of life—girls and guys at school, young adults, teachers and academics, medical students, parents, refugees, migrants, men and women. So I've been very fortunate to work in this fascinating field of healthy sexual relationships, and to support other professionals to do the same.

Personally, I've raised one beautiful, amazing girl into a fine adult (much to her credit!). I've also had my own joys, wonders and lessons about sex and relationships as I was growing up. My friends live, love, lose and love again and continue to evolve and change into strong, brave and healthy people. So I share with you what I have learned from the many girls and women who have passed their stories and experiences to me.

I want to thank all the wonderful girls who have talked with me and have advised me how it is for girls in the 21st century. The quotes are from real girls who are about your age. They are not representative of all girls, but they give us an insight and allow us to see different perspectives.

I want to thank the *Sexpectations* crew: Di, Liz, Christa (from Allen & Unwin), and my co-writer Craig, who is one of the best advocates for young people I know. I thank Chris, my partner, who shows me what real love is every day; my friends who always teach me how to love better; and my dear sister Deanne who will always be in my heart wherever we are.

I really hope this book is a guide for you in your discoveries on the journey into the wonder of love, life, joy and freedom to choose. This book is dedicated to you.

Introduction

Welcome to *Sexpectations Girl*. This book has been written for you—a girl who has expectations, or may not know *what* to expect, about sex.

Despite how much our society has changed over the years, 'sex' still causes a lot of debate because of the many meanings and ideas people attach to that simple three-lettered word, making it hard to wade through all there is to know about sex. It's sometimes difficult to work out what's right for you in a world with lots of perspectives about sex. The information, attitudes and thoughts you have about sex can make all the difference about how happy and accepting you feel about your own sexual life, and the sexual lives of other people. You'll notice in this book that we have taken what is called a 'sex-positive' approach to sex and sexuality which means that we think sex is a natural, healthy and important part of life where you make your own decisions with the best information available to you.

Knowing about sex is just as important as learning how to drive a car, or passing your school exams or even getting ready for the adventure of travelling to a new place. We don't always do these things automatically. Driving a car, passing exams and preparing to travel take preparation and practice. And sometimes we need guidance and advice to help us on our way. You need unbiased and appropriate information to make choices for this precious life of yours! *Sexpectations* is packed with information that will help you make practical sense of sex.

Sexpectations certainly talks about 'having sex'. But sex isn't just about 'doing it', although that is what a lot of people think. It is also about knowing yourself as a sexual being and the feelings and experiences this involves. Sex is a part of your life, like relationships, communication, friendship and love. This really does make sex very powerful indeed! You need to know how sex works so that it fits for you in relation to your body, mind, emotions and relationships.

Written especially for you, *Sexpectations* gives real answers to real questions that you might find hard to ask your parents or teachers. Some of you will have great teachers and friends along the way to help you through. Your parents or carers, a good friend or two, sister or maybe an adult who is important to you and who you can trust can be a guide or check-in point to learning how to make the best decisions you can.

In talking about sex, *Sexpectations* explores the most important relationship you can have: the one you have with yourself. Just keep in mind as you read that the information in this book is intended as a guide. Always consult your doctor, favourite clinician or other trusted adult in the first instance. Trust your body, trust yourself.

Chapter 1

What is Sex?

'A lot of people talk about sex but not everyone who talks about it has sex. You hear things but often they are just lying about it or they just don't know!'

'Girls are pressured to have sex to fit in.'

'Girls sometimes feel they can't win. If she wants a loving relationship and doesn't want to have sex straightaway, then she's told she is frigid by a guy. It's not fair.'

SEX IS AN ESSENTIAL AND NATURAL PART OF LIFE. Good food, fresh air and physical attention are also essential and natural. In fact, sex is everywhere if you look. Flowers do it, whales do it, people do it. It's for nurturing relationships and enjoying intimacy. It's also for pleasure and sometimes for relaxation. Sometimes, sex is for making babies. And there are as many reasons to 'have' sex as there are reasons not to have sex. You can relax, have fun and have nurturing loving relationships without having sex. Even if you don't have sex, it is still very much a part of your everyday life. Although sex is everywhere, having sex is a choice every step of the way. For some girls it's really high on the 'to do' list and for other girls it's not on their list at all. The most important thing is that when you do have sex, for the first time and any time, your reasons are right for you. We will explore first-time sex later in the book . . . stay tuned.

Why do people have sex?

When sex is mentioned, most people think of having sex as usually referring to sexual intercourse or sexual penetration. But 'being sexual' also can include other physical stuff like hugging, kissing, stroking, nuzzling and touching. It is also about feeling healthy and safe in your body, and maybe with someone else's body too. Being sexual also involves your feelings of wellbeing, excitement, lust, pleasure and joy. Sex is about your whole physical and emotional senses having a pleasurable experience. It may or may not mean having an orgasm, but it does mean feeling good with your body and your emotions.

Your sexual self is about who you are and how you feel, not just what you do. You can be and feel sexual and understand your sexuality without actually having sex. Although having sexual intercourse is or will be an important event in your whole sexual experience, it is only a part of it. Your feelings, thoughts, fantasies and exploration of your sexual identity have as much (and often more) to do with your sexual self than having sex.

'HOW DOES YOUR BODY FEEL WHEN YOU ARE HAPPY, SAD, FRIGHTENED, SAFE, TURNED ON? HOW DO DIFFERENT FEELINGS AFFECT YOUR FACIAL EXPRESSIONS, SKIN, MUSCLES, SENSE OF TENSION AND RELAXATION?'

Your body can be a signal for your feelings. Get to know and trust it. Exploring your own pleasure and sexual feelings is really to do with you feeling good about when you choose to be sexual and when you are ready to be sexual. The spectrum of your sexual feelings can be as varied as a beautiful rainbow. For example, you are experiencing your own sexual self while you are dancing or getting dressed up and ready to go out, when you're feeling attractive or checking out a good-looking guy. You might also investigate your own sexual self intimately in the privacy of your own space with masturbation (we will talk about this later). Exploring your sexual self might be with someone you like and trust in a way that makes you feel safe and happy. You might hold hands, kiss, touch or be with someone who turns on your 'inner light' and makes you feel sexually turned on (yes, more on this later too). So, being sexual is a positive and affirming part of being who you are whether you are having sex or not.

Sex and love can be a natural combination, like sand and sea, moon and stars, fresh air and sunshine. There are few things more powerful and amazing than sex and love coming together, when two people share a lot of emotional intimacy, safety, trust and physical pleasure. However, sex and love can often be confused. They are not always the same thing. You can have moon without stars and sand without sea. You can have sex without love and you can certainly have love without sex.

Some girls feel they are in love or expect to be loved because they have sex with someone. A love relationship can sometimes evolve from having sex or being sexually intimate with someone, but this doesn't often happen even if that is what a girl might want at the time.

'WHAT ARE MY VIEWS AND BELIEFS OF SEX AND LOVE?'

Some girls have told me they have had sex the first time, not because they really wanted to, but because they wanted a guy to love them or they wanted to please him and make him approve of her. Sex does not always lead to love and it also does not necessarily confer approval. This can make a girl feel quite disillusioned and invariably upset, because they are not having sex for the reasons that make them feel secure, strong and valued. Some girls I've spoken to who have had sex the first time say that they have been happy with their experience because they felt physically ready and emotionally safe.

For many girls, first-time sex just doesn't live up to the fantasy of what they expected. They've heard so much about it. What happened to the expected fireworks? What about the amazing sexual high, rush or orgasms they are supposed to get from sex the first time? After all the build-up from their friends, TV or magazines many girls say of first-time sex:

'It wasn't what I thought it would be.'
'It wasn't that big a deal but I was expecting more.'
'We rushed into it and I wondered later—why did I do that?'

They may not have been as ready as they first thought. It takes a bit of practice to feel comfortable with your body and with the intimacy that sex brings. Getting to know your body, your heart and that of someone else really does take time.

Hint: Get to practise how your body feels and responds first before you practise with someone else. Learn all you can about your own body, your mind and how to stay safe and healthy before you take the plunge. Read the *Sexpectations Boy* section. The more you know the better your decision making. Knowledge really is power.

'WHAT ARE MY FEELINGS ABOUT MY FIRST-TIME SEX EXPERIENCE? WHAT FEELINGS WILL I WANT TO HAVE? WHAT ARE MY EXPECTATIONS?'

What are the rules of the game?

People can get confused about sex when they don't get the right information. This can happen to you when you get loads of mixed-up messages or people refuse to answer your questions about sex honestly. There are plenty of rules about sex, and that can be puzzling, but many of these rules are there to protect you. Sex can be used in ways that are not always healthy, and sometimes can be very harmful, to girls. Sometimes girls experience things that they didn't really want or expect, or they were not ready for. One thing is for sure: unwanted or forced sex is not sex; it's assault and it's illegal.

There are laws related to having sex, unwanted sex and touching, and they differ between states and countries. The most consistent rules are:

» You need to reach a certain age before you can legally have sex, consent to any sexual activity, or have sex performed in front of you.
» Any sexual touching without your consent at any time is against the law.
» Sex refers to either penetration or touching a body part like the vagina, mouth, anus (or the cheeks of your bottom) and breasts. It also refers to objects being used to touch another person's body parts.
» Adults who care for you cannot have sexual contact with you while you are a child or young person under the law.

So get to know the sex laws where you live. For example, in New South Wales, Australia, you can:

- legally consent to sexual intercourse if you are 16 years of age and over;
- legally consent to a medical procedure if you are 14 years and over, as long as the clinician knows that you really understand what is involved—this includes access to some forms of contraception if the doctor decides you are mature enough, you understand the treatment, and you are not at any risk of harm or abuse;
- have access to condoms and lubricant at any age;
- have access to emergency contraception over the counter at the pharmacy, but the pharmacist needs to ask you questions to make sure you are not already pregnant and you know what this medical treatment involves; and
- get married without permission once you are 18 years of age (you can get married at 17 years of age with authority from the court or your parents).

Regardless of where you live, you have a right to:

- information and advice on sex, reproduction and protecting yourself;
- respectful relationships and safety;
- know if someone has a sexually transmissible infection (see Chapter 6: 'Safer Sex') before you have sex with them;
- say yes to legally consensual sex, depending on your age;
- say no to sex at any time;
- receive confidential treatment and consultation from a doctor or nurse;
- not be discriminated against for any reason;
- not be harassed, abused or bullied;
- seek support and advice;
- complain about how a person treats you (that might be a doctor, teacher or other person); and
- change your mind—you can make a decision and then decide that it is not what you want and this can be about having sex, kissing someone, or getting contraception (or not), or other things you make decisions about.

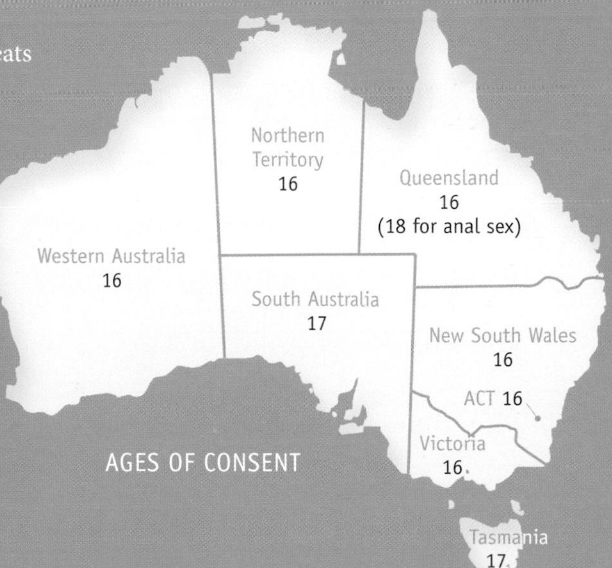

AGES OF CONSENT

How do you learn about sex?

Remember your first sex education class? I remember when I was at an all-girls' school and we had to sit with our mothers to watch a movie on reproduction and periods. I can't remember the title but I remember the feeling sitting next to my mum. She was hoping the school would address all those issues, but the school had other ideas. Needless to say, I had a wholesome education by our very forthright physical education teacher in a netball skirt and runners, who taught us the first things we needed to know. She used humour and straightforward language, and she was very approachable. I think we were very lucky to have had such a fabulous teacher but I think we were definitely in the minority.

School education on sex can sometimes be limited to reproduction, hygiene, diseases and the function of hormones. Sadly, not many people graduate with much more knowledge than their junior high school education allows them in addressing relationships and sex.

'WHAT DID YOUR SCHOOL TEACH YOU ABOUT SEX AND RELATIONSHIPS? WERE BELIEFS ABOUT SEX DISCUSSED? WHAT BELIEFS DO YOU HAVE ABOUT SEX?'

There is so much pressure on girls today to know about, talk about and even have sex, often before they are ready or before they want to. Many girls tell me they experience what they call a social 'double bind', and when it comes to sex they lose either way. They are told if they have sex, then they're a slut; and if they don't, they're frigid or a living iceberg. The pressure to behave in certain ways really can make a girl truly confused and totally stressed. Consider the following scenarios:

» The media—'Look sexy and you can have anything you want!'
» Parents and carers—'I think it's time we talk about sex' or 'Are you using condoms?' or 'Not in my house' or 'If you do it, you're out!'
» Teachers—'We only talk about it in personal development or science class' or 'Can't bear to think about it as a classroom subject!'
» Boys—'Do it or you're frigid' or 'If you love me, you wouldn't wait?'
» Other girls—'She's a slut' or 'She's frigid' or'She's all talk no action' or 'Why is she talking about it so much?'

There are some great teachers, parents, carers, guys and girlfriends who are honest and supportive (thank goodness). However, sometimes the mixed messages can be confusing and stressful to say the least. It's hard to be cool, calm and collected in making choices when you don't have all the information and there is too much feedback from other people with unhelpful personal views that are judgemental and black-and-white. Very few things in life are only one thing or another. So, take a nice deep breath, come back to yourself and try to make choices that match what *you* want and need to know for *yourself*. Take guidance from people who care about you and who you trust. Sometimes you first need to listen to your parents, teachers or carers when you are still working out what to choose for yourself.

'WHERE DO I GET POSITIVE, HELPFUL IDEAS ABOUT SEX AND SEXUALITY? WHERE DO SOME OF THE NEGATIVE THOUGHTS AND IDEAS COME FROM? WHAT ROLE DO THEY PLAY IN MY THOUGHTS ABOUT MY OWN SEXUAL SELF?'

What do we think sex is?

Girls who I've spoken to say that sex is:

'That warm feeling when you're really close and physical.'
'When you're horny.'
'Having a sexual experience with someone who turns you on.'
'What guys want most of the time!'

We can get caught up with what we think sex *should* be for girls (and guys for that matter). Sex is wonderful and exciting. It's a part of being intimate and involves deep experiences, over time, which happen through your physical and emotional being. It is about intimacy, pleasure, enjoyment and feeling ready. You can feel sexual and turned on with your imagination, or by stories you read and movies. Girls often have wonderful sexual feelings and erotic fantasies which are natural and a part of developing an understanding of sexual feelings.

Sexual boundaries can also be messy and sometimes confusing which can impact on how you feel, and sometimes think, about sex. This might happen when you feel attracted to someone but you really know it is out of your line of experience, such as being attracted to a teacher at school or your older brother's way-older friend. This might also happen when you feel attracted to someone but also confused or even weirded out by that experience because they are someone you don't really know. This might happen on the internet when you sense some attraction but you don't know who they are, or in a public venue when someone you don't know might approach you, touch you and say something flattering to you. You know you are experiencing something sexual but not sure what is happening. You might be with a group of girls, or hear a bunch of boys, who say sexual things in public, but you might not know what that means for you personally. You might feel powerful and powerless at the same time. Knowing how to respond is important in asserting what you want (and don't want) and need for yourself.

Or you might feel happy, then suddenly unhappy and you might not know why. Sometimes the changes may feel like your sex hormones have taken over the steering wheel of your life. Your body is naturally changing and, although it's probably hurtling along at a fast pace right now, it will settle into something you recognise as yours over time.

Sex can be used by some people as 'emotional currency' for approval and love. And sometimes girls think that by having sex they will keep someone close to them. However, real love is not acquired by just having sex. This is not a healthy way to experience love or sex. You will gain the best sense of security when you first start to love and respect yourself for who you are. When you feel safe and secure in yourself, sex will happen when you are happy and ready.

Raunch advertising is everywhere and tells girls what their sexuality is for them. It's a marketing tool and 'airbrushed' ad-sex is a lie that sells for profit. They are designed to catch your attention and make you want more of what they are trying to sell you. Raunch ads or video clips can make you feel sexy when you watch them. And those feelings are wonderful, exciting and natural. Feeling sexy is great. But the ads developed to sell those feelings are constructed especially to make you spend your hard-earned cash and sell a false idea of what it takes to be liked and accepted. Raunch ads are designed to make you feel bad (and then good with the product they try to sell) and suggest you aspire to an image or idea about being female that is constructed in techno-land. The images you see are not real. It's fun to watch and dance to but make sex-vertising like window-shopping—nice to look at but you don't have to have it the way it's sold to you.

'HOW DO SEX-VERTISING AND RAUNCH MUSIC VIDEOS MAKE YOU THINK AND FEEL ABOUT YOUR BODY AND SEX? WHEN YOU ARE FEELING GOOD IN YOURSELF, WHAT IMAGES COME TO YOUR MIND? WHERE DO THOSE IMAGES COME FROM?'

Lowdown on porn

We often hear of pornography without always understanding what it is. It's generally accepted that pornography consists of writing, pictures or video that have no artistic value other than to stimulate sexual desire or excitement. It's widely debated where the border exists between artistic expression and where erotic art verges on the pornographic. Some of the earliest created images of art have some sexual connotation and interpretation. This says that human expression has involved sexual ideas from the earliest days of artistic development. If images have been produced with purely erotic and pornographic intention, then it can often only be understood in the context of the time and society it was produced. Feminists and liberalists both oppose and support each other's views in different arguments on porn. It's hotly debated and there is little consensus about its value or use in relation to sex.

That being said, we have our own current social and cultural standards of what is understood to be acceptable. I am not saying that porn, of itself, is either bad or good. You need to make those decisions for yourself and understand the social rules of pornography and sexual imagery in our society. There is a lot of bad porn out there that is way too easy to access on the net. There are laws about accessing porn. If you have access to porn images then use your judgement and ask—does this porn show someone being treated as an object? Does it break the rules regarding age and consent? Does a woman look like she is genuinely okay with what is going on? Basically, any porn that involves or shows a person not consenting to sexual activity is degrading and not okay. Porn that involves animals or girls and boys under age is illegal, abusive and definitely wrong.

Porn can often create confusion about what constitutes natural or 'normal' sex: the sex people have without endless re-takes and an editing suite. Porn can set girls up into thinking that the only good sex that exists is porn-sex. And they consequently (and wrongly) believe that the only sexually acceptable girl is a porn star. The reality is that porn-sex is not real sex—it's made-up sex in a studio with a camera person, a director, a studio-lighting person, hours of re-takes, bad breath, farts, smells, false moaning, rashes, a make-up person for those rashes, not being sexually aroused, and lots of editing. It is said by some people that porn offends and degrades women because it's designed and created by men to degrade and subjugate women for their pleasure. There is also female erotica (sexually explicit material) designed for women that is said to maintain their dignity and arouse sexual desire. Female erotica displays sexual encounters that are intended to enhance women's experience and not put women down or make them an object of a guy's sexual outlet. Let's face it, sexual enjoyment really is not just a guy's privilege. Girls are entitled to their own understanding, responses and ways of achieving their own sexual desire and excitement without having mainstream porn as a model of sexual normality. And guys need another way of seeing girls' sexual responses in a light other than that shone on the porn industry. Negotiating if, and how, porn is used in your relationship is really important. You are entitled to know if your boyfriend uses porn. You also need to acknowledge your own sexual expression that may, and may not, include ideas established by porn images. And you can establish your natural sexual self whether porn asserts a standard or not about sexual behaviour.

Sexpectations Boy has a great section on porn. Just flip the book over and have a read.

'WHAT NEGATIVE THOUGHTS DO I HAVE ABOUT MY BODY AND WHERE DO THEY COME FROM? WHAT POSITIVE THOUGHTS DO I HAVE ABOUT MY BODY?'

SEX IS

Consensual—It requires your say-so at every step of the way and you can change your mind at any point.

Creative—It's about enjoyment. If you're not enjoying it, you shouldn't be doing it.

Communication—Trusting talk and open communication are a big part of sex, including body language, cyber-sex and phone sex.

Contact—Sex is safe, positive contact between people in the most physically intimate way.

Choice—You get to choose if and when you have sex, and with whom.

SEX IS NOT

Forced—When someone tries to have sex against someone's will: this is assault or rape; it isn't sex.

Just for creating babies—Sex is experienced all over the world for lots of reasons, making babies being only one of them.

Just about orgasms—An orgasm can be a great experience but people can have great sex without having an orgasm. People can have an orgasm without having great sex. (Who said sex was simple!)

Just about someone else and what the other person wants.

TRICKY QUESTIONS

Q **Isn't sex only about having babies?**

A Sex is not always about reproduction, just as it's not always about love and commitment. For many people, their religious, cultural and personal experiences can be a big influence on whether to have sex or not, and for the reasons they choose to have sex. Some people say they choose to be married first before they have sex. But sex can be defined in different ways; some people are having sexual encounters when they think they are not—like oral sex or mutual masturbation. So having sexual intercourse is likely to involve reproduction, but sexual experiences generally do not necessarily mean babies will be born. But no matter what others say, think or feel, whether or not you have sex must be a decision you make that is right for you.

Q **Will having sex make me popular?**

A If you think other people are doing it because they think it's very cool, then think again. Some people are, some aren't and some people lie about doing it. Teenagers are not always having as much sex as they claim. Having sex as an attempt for social approval, sadly, will probably backfire. If having sex is something you are ready for, then it won't matter what other people think when that time comes. It could be a deeply personal, private and safe experience that you only share with someone you trust, you may have sex in a public place like a party, you may be talking about having it or you may choose not to have sex yet for a range of good reasons. Whichever way you choose, sex is not a popularity contest because, in the end, most people will have some sexual experience at some point in their life. Learn all you can now so you can make the right decision for you.

Q **Everyone is doing it: no one is choosing to delay sex any more, so why should I?**

A This may surprise you, but more young people today are choosing to delay their first sexual experience. Although some girls have told me that oral sex is more common than penetrative sex, it is more common now to say 'not yet' than it was in your parents' generation, because girls felt they had less personal choices then about how they responded to sexual pressure. Remember, when you choose to have sex does not have to rely on what other people say they are doing. It's your decision.

‘WHAT DO I THINK SEX IS, AND WHAT INFLUENCES WHAT I BELIEVE?’

Chapter 2

Body Bits

'There are plenty of girls who don't know about sex. They don't know about their bodies and stuff and no one talks to them about it.'

'The best thing about sex? . . . Feeling comfortable in your own body and having an orgasm!'

'Schools reckon they give us what we need to know. They talk about safe sex but they don't talk about sex.'

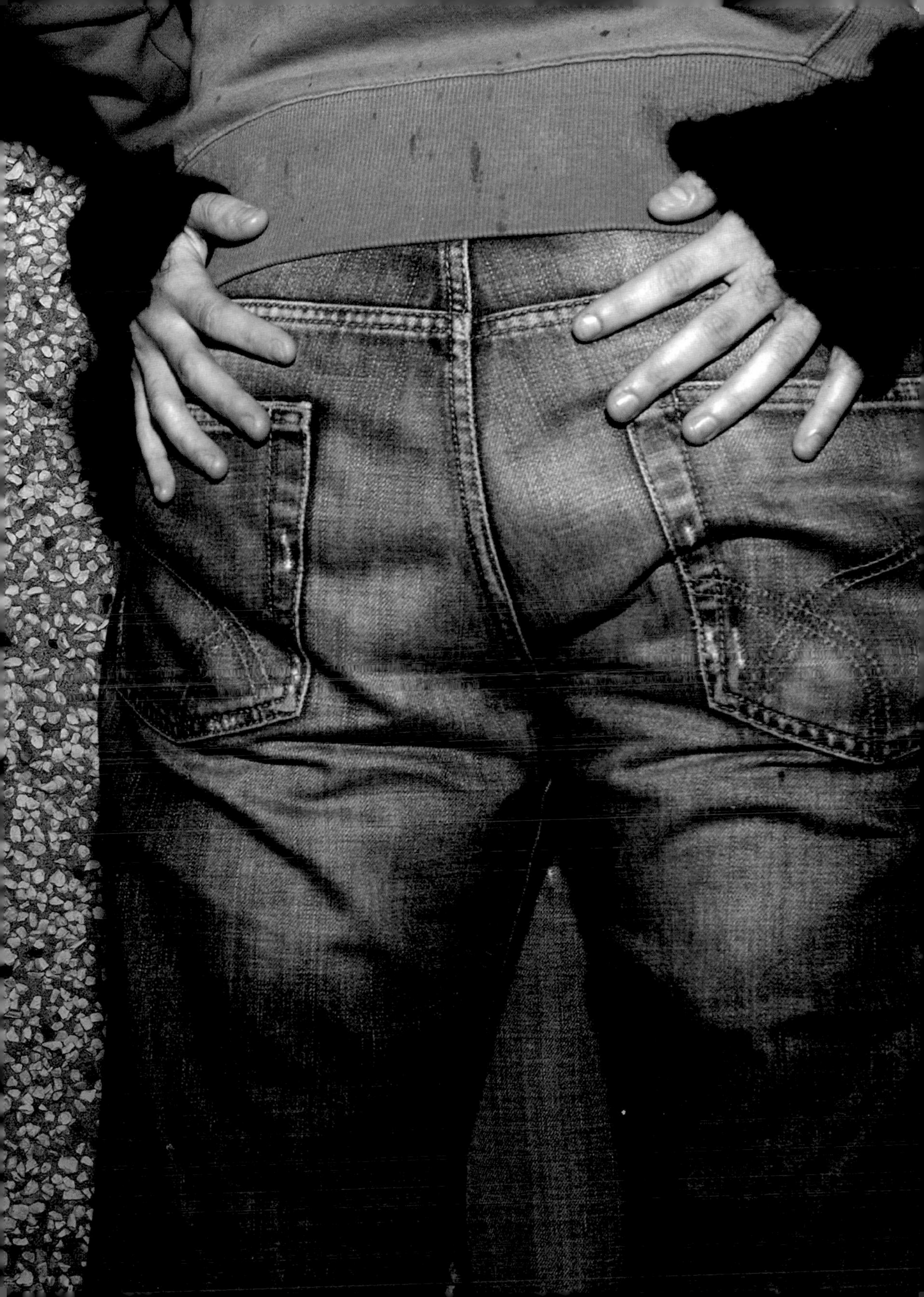

In the last couple of years you will have noticed your body blossom, seemingly out of nowhere. Boobs, bumps and 'little-bum fluff' appearing without warning. Welcome to puberty!

This *is* the biggest, quickest change your body will ever experience, which can feel a bit freaky. But if it didn't happen what would that be? Even more freaky! Changes do take time to get used to and what you are experiencing will feel so normal after a while that you'll wonder what you were worried about.

When hormones kick in

The most important sex organ in the whole body is your brain. It's doing some wild stuff in the time you're transmuting from teen to queen! Your pituitary gland (in the brain) releases hormones that set off a chain reaction in the rest of your body. It's because of this that you start to develop all the physical and emotional signs of growing up.

When you meet someone you like in *that* way, there are a million things buzzing around your body and across the crowded room. Emotions are linked to your hormones like trains on a track. In your own body, hormones can really make you feel excited and sexual or relaxed and zoned out. Have you noticed that when someone is 'in love' around you, say a friend or your sister, that you somehow feel just a little bit 'in love' too? You are experiencing the other person's pheromones, or sex hormones, which are released in the air. Feeling 'in love' is really related to hormones and is the best natural high you can have for free and with no side-effects!

There is a bunch of hormones produced by your body that sends all kinds of signals. You know the attraction feelings: excited, a bit anxious, loads more energy, flushed, warm, sweaty, and your heart gets all fluttery! Oxytocin is one of those hormones produced in the brain and it is a chemical dynamo. It is part of the sexual arousal response and it helps you bond to others. It's the 'rush' chemical that makes you feel like you can do anything! Adrenalin also plays a big role—it's the stuff that really keeps you buzzing; the way feeling 'in love' can.

When sexual arousal hormones kick in at full blast, your breasts can increase in size (a real natural boob job!), you can become more wet (it's vaginal fluid, not pee) and sweaty in the nether regions, and there is an arousal of the clitoris. All this is happening in parts of the body you may not have even thought about before! What are these bits? You might get a little brave and check out what parts of your body look like. It's okay and actually normal to look at your body and see what's happening. It is, after all, your body. Find somewhere private and, with a little mirror, see for yourself.

Your reproductive system or 'your bits'

Let's talk about 'down there'. Lots of girls may have covered this topic at school but some haven't. There's no test here; this is a super-quick overview just to make sure you have the facts.

When you look at the area outside your vagina, you'll see folds of skin called the vulva. If you look a little further inside, there are two layers of pink skin—thick (outside) and thin (inside). These are your labia. And right at the top, under a fold of skin, is the clitoris, with plenty of nerve endings to make it sensitive, and it has no other purpose than to make you feel good and sometimes lead to orgasm—a bonus! For more about the clitoris see 'Thank you, Mother Nature'.

The first little hole is the urethra, which is for letting your pee out. It's really small so you might not be able to see it.

Then there's the entrance to your vagina—a magnificent work of nature. The vagina is extremely flexible (which is why a baby can pass through during birth), muscular (to help with birth and having sex), and has few nerve endings. The vagina is as long as your middle finger. Things can go into a vagina: a tampon, speculum (for pap smears, a medical test), penis, finger or sex toy for pleasure. Things can also come out of a vagina: mucus, blood, fluid and uterine lining from a period, and babies.

You might notice a bit of skin around the inside of your vagina—a bit like the rolled-up sleeve of a shirt or bits of very thin tissue-like skin. This is likely to be your hymen. Don't worry if you don't have one. If you do, it will rarely completely cover your vagina. If it does, you might need to have it checked by a doctor to make sure you can menstruate (have your period) through it. For information on the hymen, see the box 'What is a hymen?.'

Right inside and up into your vagina is the cervix (if feels like the tip of your nose if you touch it with the end of your finger), which is the entrance to your uterus (womb). The uterus is the protective cradle for a developing baby until it's born.

On the outside, the last little bit towards your back is your anus (your bottom), where faeces (poo) come out.

THANK YOU, MOTHER NATURE

The epicentre of female orgasm is the clitoris. The clitoris feels like a very sensitive knob at the top of your vulva. Its only known purpose is to give a girl pleasure. With the right stimulation of the clitoris, this area tenses up and fills with blood. Orgasm is the physical release after this tension. The clitoris is a lot bigger than people think. We know now that the clitoris has about the same number of nerve endings as a guy's penis but in a much smaller space, which makes it incredibly sensitive. These nerves extend right into the pelvic area. Touching it can be sensitive and very pleasurable and is the most common way a girl can reach orgasm. The use of personal lubricant or saliva while rubbing the clitoris reduces friction during stimulation and increases sensitivity.

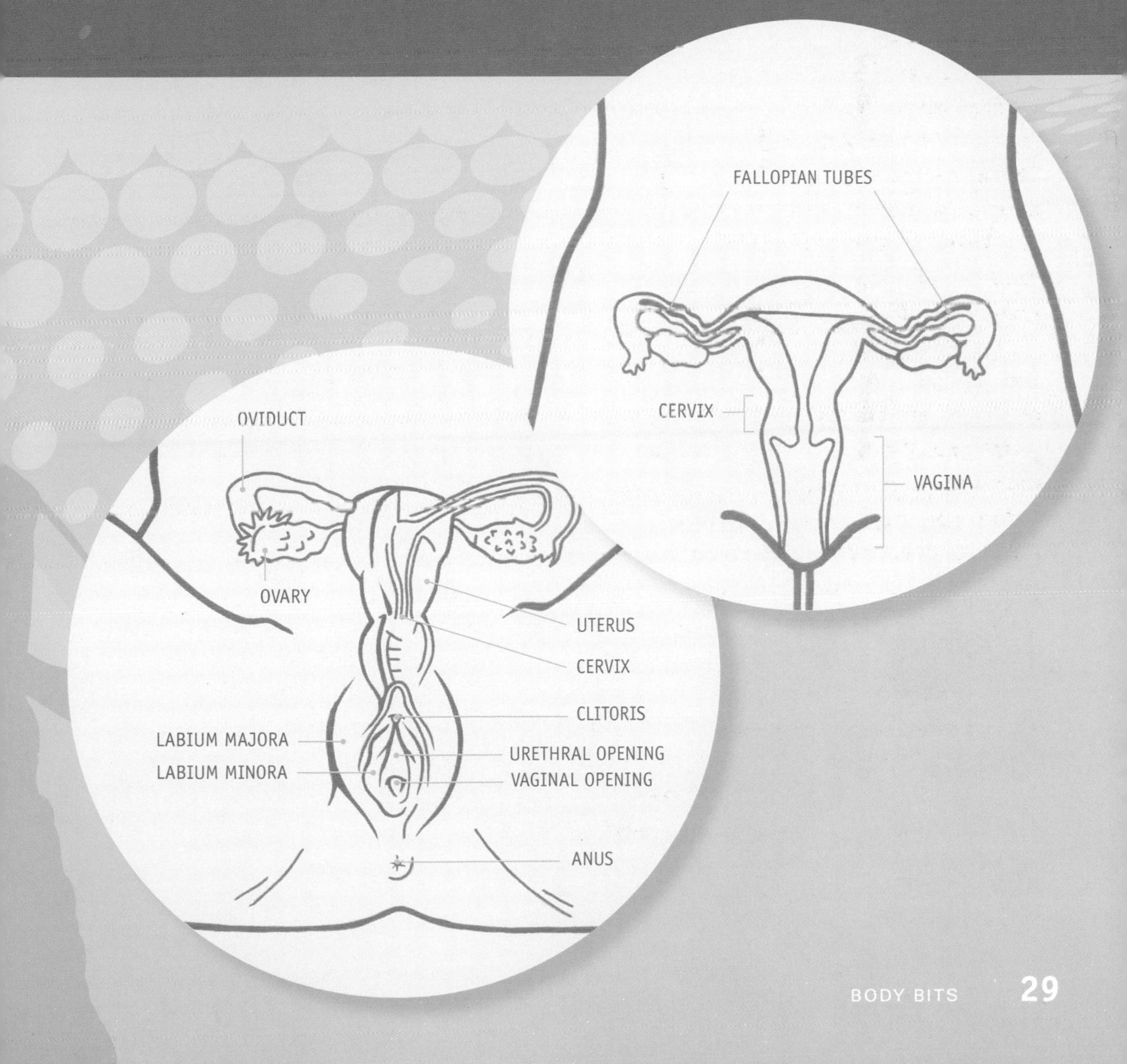

Pleasure and your body

Pleasure is one of the main reasons many people have sex. The enjoyment of intimacy, feeling someone else's body close to them, and the sensual experiences of touch, taste and smell are highlights of sexual experience. Girls (and guys) often think that sex is about orgasm alone but it's just one part of the picture. Anyway, I know you've heard about it before, so let's talk about the Big O first and then talk about your body and pleasure you can experience in other ways.

ORGASM

Orgasm, also called 'coming', 'cumming' or 'climax', is the feel-good 'rush' towards the end of sexual stimulation. It can feel like a radiating sensation or release from the sexual areas to the rest of your body. Orgasm can be noisy or quiet, a sense of a huge explosion or a warm flow of warmth. Some women can have more than one orgasm and some women do not have any orgasms. Orgasm can be a different experience for everybody. There is no 'right' way to feel or experience it. But trust, safety and exploration are really, really important in a girl's sexual experience.

Girls can experience orgasm in a lot of different ways. For lots of girls, experiencing orgasm is about relaxing, physically releasing and letting go. But for a lot of guys, it's the opposite and often about a build-up of energy. Often alcohol or drugs actually reduce the potential for an orgasm.

Your brain is the organ that produces hormones responsive to orgasm. It responds to sexual stimuli by relaxing some parts of the body and tensing other parts. So while the genital and pelvic area relaxes and engorges with blood, the heart is racing, breathing gets heavier and the body is feeling excited! When you feel sexually aroused, blood fills your pelvic area and fluid lines the vagina, making it slippery. Your breasts also increase in size with sexual arousal. The nipples become erect and can be very sensitive to touch. Some women can even experience an orgasm with nipple stimulation.

Despite common belief, it is not often that women orgasm from vaginal intercourse alone because there are not many nerve endings in the vagina to adequately stimulate a heightened sexual response. There is the G-spot (well, it's not really a spot, it's more of an area) at the front of the vaginal wall, inside your body. If you lie on your back, it's on the top part of your vagina. Some women can orgasm if this area is stimulated enough, and the most likely way for that to happen is during sexual intercourse when the girl is on top (read more about positions in Chapter 5).

Direct clitoral stimulation is the most common way for a girl to orgasm and, on average, this can take anything from two to 20 minutes or so. This means you can build up to it and enjoy the process at the same time. While guys can sometimes be faster at reaching orgasm, a girl's orgasm can last longer than a guy's. But that's all generally speaking. What about you? Do you know what makes you feel good?

The skin can be a sexual organ all over! The skin often flushes when aroused, which can sometimes look like a rash on the cheeks and chest. Don't worry though, it will subside with time. Kissing, touching and licking can be very sexual, especially in sensitive body areas like the neck, earlobes, the inner part of the wrist, behind the knees . . . you name it! Knowing your erogenous zones takes a little exploration on your own and a dose of trust, communication and patience with someone with whom you want to be physically intimate.

Men generally release semen (with sperm) when they have an orgasm (see the boys' section for more on this). Women are known to also release fluid in small quantities but generally they'll experience quick muscular contractions, a feeling of tension and then release—an all-body 'wash' of pleasure or euphoria. The feeling after an orgasm can really be different for different girls. Some girls experience a huge crazy rush, and some feel a warm tingling flow. It's totally different for every girl and it needs to be because you are an individual. How long it takes to reach an orgasm can also vary depending on how relaxed and turned on a woman feels, how familiar her sexual partner is with her body, and what kind of sexual activity is occurring.

WHAT IS A HYMEN?

The hymen is a very thin membrane that surrounds the outer part of the vagina and it serves no particular biological function. Most girls are born with an incomplete hymen; that is, it does not cover the vagina entirely as there is usually a natural hole in it. It's usually very thin and tissue-like in texture so it is common for the hymen to break or stretch as a girl is growing up and being naturally active. It is rare for a tampon to 'break' the hymen since it usually has a hole in it already.

There is a belief in some cultures that the hymen is an indicator of a girl's virginity. But it is very difficult to determine if a girl is a virgin simply from examining the hymen. About one in 2000 women will have a 'complete' hymen that covers their vagina and may need a doctor to break it and allow menstrual blood to flow out.

DID YOU KNOW?

The word 'hymen' means 'skin' or 'membrane' in Greek. It was a word used to describe all kinds of membranes in the body, not just over the vagina entrance.

What's normal about normal?

Sometimes it's easy to get caught up in the idea of what is normal simply because it is usually based on someone's idea of what it means and ignores the value of natural diversity. Often, there is no such thing as 'normal', but there is certainly such as a thing as healthy and unhealthy. I certainly like to think of variations in our bodies, minds and activities in terms of these two questions:

- Is what I am experiencing in my body, mind or activities generally healthy?
- Does my experience with my body, mind and activities generally support my health and promote my own, or others', wellbeing?

If you answered no to these questions, then I'd suggest you will need assistance and support to work out and change what stops you from being healthy. For those of you who are still thinking about what might or might not be considered normal with your body, then let's talk about this a little.

'WHERE DO YOU GET YOUR IDEA OF "NORMAL" FROM?'

Body fluids are something a lot of girls feel uncomfortable about. But they are a part of our everyday lives and we would be crinkly and rusty without them, and here's the lowdown so you know what to expect.

YOUR MENSTRUAL CYCLE

The menstrual cycle is when the body prepares once a month for the possibility of pregnancy. The average menstrual cycle is 28 days, although it is very, very common and generally normal for girls to have irregular cycles or a different cycle from 24 to 35 days. Using the average cycle as an example, this is what is likely to be happening inside your body during those 28 days:

Day 1—Bleeding (period) starts. It's a mixture of blood, uterine lining, tissue fluid and mucus, and it passes from the uterus to the cervix to the vagina and out. The uterus might cramp a little during this time. The normal amount of blood lost during a period is about two tablespoons.

Days 3 to 5—Period stops. By this time about 20 or so little ovary follicles (like egg cups), each holding eggs or ovum, have been growing in the last few days.

Days 6 to 13—The eggs grow and the race is on to see which one gets to be released. During this time the uterus is re-lining itself, becoming ready for a fertilised egg to attach to it, like a little bed.

Day 14—You are at your most fertile around 14 to 16 days before the end of your menstrual cycle. That's right, you need to count backwards from the end of the cycle, and you won't know exactly when that is, which is why it's a little tricky to pinpoint when you are fertile. At this time your pituitary gland in your brain releases hormones that allow the ripest egg to be released by the ovary. The released egg is carried by thousands of assistant cells and swept along the fallopian tube, ready to meet the sperm (there's more on sperm in the boys' section and it's good to know about this, so flip over and read up). The most fertile time lasts around 24 hours, and during this time the cervical mucus discharged from your vagina becomes clear, thin and sticky.

Days 15 to 28—The lining of your uterus thickens for a week after ovulation. If the sperm and egg meet, the now 'fertilised ovum' will cruise down the fallopian tube for a few days before it snuggles into the bed of the uterus. If there is no fertilisation or implantation, then the uterine lining starts to deteriorate—this eventually results in a period (back to Day 1). At this point, the ovaries are starting to pump up the hormones in preparation for maturing a new egg.

DID YOU KNOW?

The human egg, or ovum, is a voluptuous big girl of the cell world—it is one cell that can be seen with the naked eye, just! It is also like a queen, in that it has a group of 'nurse' cells that cluster around the ovum to protect and care for it before it is released. When a baby girl is born, she has more than a million primitive egg cells in her ovaries, but will only have a few hundred thousand by the time she hits puberty. Humans and great apes (chimps and gorillas, for example) have periods or menstrual bleeding. All other female mammals re-absorb the uterine lining back into their body.

MUCUS

Girls naturally produce mucus in their vagina. It keeps your vagina healthy and it changes during the month from a clear, thin but sticky fluid to a thicker, yellowy gluey mucus towards period time. Having mucus or clear stuff in your undies is normal since the vagina is spring-cleaning each month. If you have mucus that is unusually smelly or has blood or is a different colour, it can be a sign of an infection. Girls can have infections in their urinary tract or vagina without having had sex. So, if you're worried, I'd suggest you go to a doctor to get it checked out.

Being sexually turned on brings out the best of our body fluids. For girls, their vagina normally oozes a clear, slippery fluid. Some women have a feeling of ejaculating fluid when they feel sexually stimulated. Science now knows this is not urine but a unique fluid produced by the female prostate-like gland. Girls and guys are more similar than we thought!

SWEAT

Sweat is sexy and natural. It can contain pheromones that are natural sex 'perfumes' to arouse the sexual senses. If someone smells nice to you (their natural smell, not deodorant or after shave), then that can play a big part in sexual attraction. Don't lose touch with your body signs. Keep in tune with your senses.

'DO I KNOW ALL THERE IS TO KNOW ABOUT MY BODY BITS?'

TRICKY QUESTIONS

Q **How do I know if a penis will fit into my vagina?**

A All guys and girls are different and there is no 'normal' penis or vagina size. A penis changes from when it is flaccid (soft) to when it is erect (hard). (Read more about this in the guys' section.) Your vagina is muscular and flexible. This means it can expand easily during sexual intercourse and, later, during childbirth. Vaginal fluid released from the vagina makes it slippery and easier to have sex. Feeling anxious or stressed can make the vaginal muscles tighten. When having sex, being in control of the way you move can be useful in relaxing the muscles, and this can be done by you being on top during sex (with the guy being underneath and you kneeling on either side), or stopping when it feels uncomfortable. You can also use a water-based lubricant to make things more slippery (and more comfortable).

Q **Why would my periods stop?**

A Sometimes a girl's period will stop for a range of reasons totally unrelated to pregnancy. She might be totally stressed over an extended period of time, or she might have lost too much weight and her hormones have gone into 'starvation mode' (that is, turned down the biological heater to minimise any losses). Periods also might stop because she is doing heaps of sport and not eating enough nutritious food. However, if you have had unprotected sex recently, it might also indicate a pregnancy.

Q **How can you tell if someone's a virgin?**

A A virgin is someone who is sexually inexperienced. Sexual experience can mean many things, but it usually means a consensual form of intercourse whether that is oral, vaginal, anal or mutual masturbation. However, the terminology can be widely debated. Historically (such as 1200 AD or so), the word 'virgin' had been specifically applied to sexually inexperienced young girls, but this definition has more recently evolved to include older girls and boys. Social views thankfully are slowly changing. Some cultures and languages actually have a specific word for male virginity! There is no test for virginity and you cannot tell by looking if someone is a virgin. Many young people do not find it embarrassing to say they are virgins.

Q **Will using a tampon mean I'm not a virgin anymore?**

A A tampon is not about being sexually active but is designed as a hygiene product. When used properly and changed frequently, it is a normal, healthy way to capture menstrual blood when you have your period. Using a tampon does not mean a loss of virginity.

Chapter 3

You, Your Mind and Sex

'Sex isn't a big deal anymore and it's not what it's made out to be.'

'Some girls think that when their boyfriend breaks up with them, it's the end of the world. They don't know how to act. They just give up. They really put that on themselves.'

'What's important? A sense of purpose. Friendships are really important. Going to parties, hanging out. School work and doing well, but that depends on your personality. I want to be free and not tied down with a relationship. So I'm taking my time.'

Body image

Exploring your body is a good way of understanding how it naturally and magically fluctuates. All the cells of every part of your body are rejuvenating and being replaced over the whole time of your growing-up years and beyond. During puberty and your teenage years, your body is going through its greatest change of all; that is, unless you become pregnant or start to experience menopause. This is when your hormones and fertility changes as an older woman and usually starts from late 40 to 50 years of age but varies for each woman. You are changing all the time and growing in ways your body and mind are just needing to get used to, so give your body, and your mind, a rest from the onslaught of negative criticism.

Remember:

» A woman's body is naturally curvy with an important fat layer on parts of your body, no matter what weight you are.

» It's normal for your weight to fluctuate every week.

» Most (real) guys do *not* want to get involved with the likes of underwear models—maybe in their dreams, but not in real life.

» Unrealistic expectations, such as trying to be model-thin, can make you feel, act and look hollow and empty—very *not* sexy—and can make you feel depressed.

Girls come in a variety of fabulous shapes, sizes and personal styles. You don't need to model yourself on collagen-pumped and botoxed wanna-be starlets. You already have your own special wow factor. Look around and you'll see many really cool, smart, together girls who have their own unique style. You can be your role model and practise a positive style sense. Get in touch with your own beautiful girl inside you.

Think about what you want to project out into the world about yourself. Develop a sense of your own personal taste in clothes, music and what you like. If you really want to give that wow impression, no amount of copying will do it. That's because it's a secret thing that exists only in *you*. You can find it with some research into your own personal self-image that's yours alone. When you wear clothes and make-up that are naturally you, your inner glow will shine out. Genuine beauty is naturally gorgeous, not necessarily expensive glamour.

The most important thing is to be true to yourself. When you feel confident, comfortable and happy, this is beautiful. No amount of make-up or cleavage will beat the beauty of your smile and your everyday living joy.

Getting 'in touch' with your body

Okay, so let's talk masturbation. Masturbation is sexual stimulation and arousal with yourself. Why do you do it? Well, it's a way to release sexual steam safely, and it's a healthy part of a person's sexual life. Both girls and boys can masturbate; it can be done while sitting, standing or lying down; and it's the one true 'safe sex'.

Some girls masturbate to orgasm. If you want to try masturbating, the important thing is to feel pleasure in a private place and to get to know how your body responds and what it likes in a sexually pleasurable way, whether you orgasm or not. Some societies and cultures have rules that make it seem like masturbation is bad, rude or wrong. There were once strange beliefs about masturbation, like your hands would grow hair or you would go blind. We know these ideas are not true.

Touching your body and exploring your feelings are normal and natural things to do. Learning about touching is a way of also sensing your own safe boundaries and it is a good way to discover what feels comfortable, safe and good for you. In fact, little children often naturally touch and fondle their genitals while they are sleeping or as a way of comforting themselves and exploring their bodies. So touching yourself is something you knew as a child and it's a very natural thing to do.

Embracing the single you

Being a single girl is perfectly normal, fun, creative and free. There's a lot of pressure to be hooked up with someone in a world seemingly *filled* with couply types. It can feel like others want to see you with just anyone else because it makes them feel uncomfortable to see a single person around them. The message out there seems to be that you can only ever expect to be half a person if you are single. We know in our hearts it's not true, but some girls believe that they are not valuable unless they are in a relationship. There are other more important ways of defining your personal value other than seeing yourself through someone else.

Remember, all girls have been single before, many girls are single now and plenty of girls will be single again later on. After all, you've got a long time to live with you! So make the most of the time on your own, explore being independent and self-directed, and get in tune with yourself. Spend time with people who are supportive, care about who you are and bring smiles to your beautiful face. Your everyday life is a wonderful place to practise being spontaneous, gorgeous, generous, calm and to shine from your heart! No one but you can give you that inner beauty and joy.

Relationships might come and go but things like good friends, doing what you love and having a plan for your future can always be there. In fact, you need to always make these a part of your life whether you are with someone or whether you are single. After a break-up, your self-esteem might take a blow, especially if your 'singles' muscles are a little on the flabby side and you can't see the bottom of the emotional swimming pool of life. But that is the time to get yourself back in shape and become strong again for the adventures yet to come!

Unless you work out what it is that makes being single great for you, you won't really know what's so fabulous about being with someone else who is truly worth it. Being single sometimes takes training. You need to build those emotional 'singles' muscles. Practising being single is a great opportunity to embrace YOU and to do the things you really need to do for your future. Knowing yourself and what you want in life means you won't just settle for whoever comes swaggering your way, but will actually choose the right person and relationship for you.

'WHAT ARE THREE THINGS THAT YOU CAN DO ON YOUR OWN THAT YOU LOVE?'

TRICKY QUESTIONS

Q **I think I like guys but I am also attracted to a girl at school. I feel confused. What should I do?**

A Exploring and getting to know your own sexuality, or who you are attracted to, can be transforming and liberating experience. But there are times when it can also be confusing. If you feel attracted to someone else, it may be a guy or a girl, or both, this can feel wonderful, challenging or confusing. You might ask the question 'Is this normal?' or 'Is there someone else like me?' Exploring your feelings sometimes can feel exciting, but it can also feel confronting due to the judgements people make about what is normal and not normal. However, what we are shown to be 'normal' and taught in school and home is not always natural or true for some girls. Also what we are taught as 'normal' is either one person's idea or a social construct of what is normal. This idea of normal varies across the world. If you are feeling confused or unsure, you need to take time to seek good advice and affirming support, knowing that, with a little patience and courage on your part, you will get clearer about what's natural and normal for you as your sexual attraction unfolds over time. Remember that diversity is natural, and sexual diversity is important and it is naturally evident in every corner of the world.

'HOW DO I SEE MY SEXUALITY AND AM I OKAY WITH IT?'

Q I've heard about masturbation but how do I 'do' it?

A Masturbation is something to do in private (like your bedroom or while you are having a bath). You can consider practising by using your fingers and feeling your front genital area gently with pressure. If you are more adventurous you could insert your finger into your vagina and press gently to the front of the vagina. Girls also find fondling their vagina, especially the inside of the front part, very pleasurable. The most important thing is to simply relax and think about your sexual desires and see where they take you. Fantasy and imagination can be fun while masturbating. Your clitoris and breasts are sensual erotic parts; taking it slow and steady by stroking or playing with them can be very erotic.

Rubbing and fondling yourself through bed clothing and pillows can also be exciting. Some girls like water pressure from the shower on their clitoris, and you can experiment by changing the pressure and speed of your stimulation and see what works for you.

Listen to your body and follow it. Don't be rough with yourself and don't give yourself a hard time if it's not what you imagined. Remember, it takes a little practice and some patience. And if you don't like it then that is perfectly all right too.

Q I don't like the idea of sex. I can't imagine doing it. Am I normal?

A It's perfectly normal not to want to have sex at different times and stages of your life. Every person is different and has their own pace of development. It's important you don't do anything you don't want to do. We all grow up with family, social and cultural ideas about sex, so think about the values you have about sex and where they come from. These may also change over time depending on your own experience. Some social and moral values suggest that sex is a 'bad' or 'forbidden' thing, which can inhibit acceptance of sex as a normal and natural part of life. Being sexual is not just 'having sex' with someone—sexuality is part of everyone even when they aren't having sex! Feeling comfortable in your body and feeling emotionally alive is important to having a sexual self. Focus on your self-happiness first. 'Sex' will work itself out for you eventually.

Chapter 4

The First Time—Lust, Love 'n' All That

'It's good when there's a balance. You have to not be afraid to voice your own opinion. When a guy makes an effort to like my friends, I like that. He values my relationships.'

'Most girls plan on having a long-term relationship down the track. They have long-term plans of kids and marriage.'

'I've got friends who are a good couple. They are annoying—she is my best friend and I only see her at school now. His friends complain they never see him too. But they like each other and they've chosen to be together. So it's cool.'

First love is intense! It's when we 'fall in love' for the first time. Kapow! It's deeper than lust but feels out of our control. First love may or may not be with someone you have sex with. But they are special enough to put the word 'love' to. That's pretty special!

Lust is a very powerful sexual feeling. It is the sister of passion and sex. In the beginning, lust is easily confused with love. Lust often 'flames up' but then it goes out quickly. In a relationship, love is the 'slow burn' and not always a whiz-bang, short-fuse experience.

Lust can also be very much a part of a longer term relationship; balanced with love and communication, it can be a very powerful and fulfilling combination.

A crush is when your body and mind are practising to love romantically. It can feel like love but it's really just made up. It is a strong attraction to someone you cannot really share that with. You might have a crush on a teacher, someone on the bus, a friend, a friend's brother, your sister's boyfriend, a girl at school, a pop star or movie actor. It's normal to have fantasies, sexual or otherwise, about all kinds of people, but just not always cool to try to act on them—say, with a teacher or pop star. They are just fantasies and they will change over time.

So the experiences of a crush, lust and love can be quite different and it's important to know the difference. When you start feeling attracted to someone, these feelings can be confusing because they might all come together in a big rush.

You might think you are falling in love but really be experiencing a full-on crush with lust thrown in for good measure. And these can be heady wonderful feelings that can take us on a slippery slide of sexual options. You might go head first into wanting to be with someone sexually and start by kissing them. Woohoo! But is it lust, love or a crush? You decide.

When you have kissed someone, it doesn't mean you have to have sex or progress to other sexual activity. You may want to have lots of kisses before you feel comfortable and become more sexual. You need to be prepared before the lust flames take over and other sexual opportunities appear. It can happen very quickly sometimes, so you need to have your COMFY list to stay ahead and in control:

C Clear head; alcohol and drugs are not a good friend at this time.

O Open mind; keep questioning if you need to stop or stay.

M Moments to stop and think; AM I READY?

F Friends close by; never be too far away from them when you are with your guy.

Y Your condoms and lube, just in case.

If things go further and you've said yes to sex, you CAN still change your mind at any time after that. You are not wrong, bad, a tart or a come-on. You just changed your mind. You need to be respected if and when you change your mind. Don't be anywhere where your friends can't get you if it gets too hot to handle. Making the decision to have sex for the first time is an important one.

Sex is more than doing it. It's a huge decision and one that you should only make when you are well and truly ready. What do you feel when you think about sex? Thrilled, scared, strong, challenged, happy, relieved, worried, nervous, anxious, good, joyous, amazed, bliss, crazy, confused, neutral, okay, numb, bad, attractive, sexy, assaulted, loving, connected, weak, disappointed? There is a range of feelings that girls have—and all of them are right. The most important thing to remember is that your feelings are an important part of you and they will also change like you do. You may not feel all of them at once, but being sexual can bring out these feelings across the spectrum of your life as a natural part of your experience as you grow older. When you need assistance and help with any of these feelings and experiences, you can find it with your good friends, parents or carers, other positive support people, a counsellor or reliable websites to help you work towards your own strength and independence.

Are you ready?

So, the scene is set and you think you're ready. You're with your boyfriend and you really like him and you feel horny and things are getting steamy and damp. The next step is full-blown sex—for sure. You can feel it.

But wait!

Before you dive in, it's important to check in with yourself:

» Are you with someone who arouses you *and* makes you feel safe?
» Are you comfortable with your own body?
» Can you tell your partner how you feel and be comfortable doing so?
» Do you get loads of positive vibes?
» Do you share a good laugh? (Sex *can* be hilarious!)
» Are you having sex because you want to?
» Do you have a safe, private place to go to?
» Do you have condoms and plenty of lubrication, and possibly other contraception?
» Have you talked about prevention (you know, pregnancy and STIs) ?

A lot of questions, yes, but it's a good checklist to make sure you are positive this is what *you* want. And before we leave it there, try the 'Quiz—Is this right for me?'

QUIZ—IS THIS RIGHT FOR ME?

By circling your answer to the question, you can read more to help you work out where you're at with first-time sex.

1. THE BEST REASON TO HAVE FIRST-TIME SEX IS BECAUSE:

A I'm happy and secure in myself and want to share with this person.
B I'm curious about how it feels and know I can handle it.
C I'm bored and lonely.
D I'm the only virgin on the block.

A Sex is about sharing good feelings of being happy and secure in yourself, and having someone respect you for who you are. It's not about what you can do for them.
B Curiosity can often lead to first-time sex, but it's probably not a good reason on its own. However, if you're happy in yourself and trust the relationship you're in, it's a way to explore with someone you trust.
C Being bored or lonely is the worst possible reason to have first-time sex—mainly because it's a ticket to more boredom and loneliness down the track. There are more inspired things to do when boredom and loneliness strike.
D Sometimes first-time sex comes from sexual pressure from other people. Sex is not a competition and choosing not to have sex is normal. Only you know when you're ready.

2. THE PERSON I'VE GOT MY EYE ON:

A Is great! We laugh and talk and we understand each other.
B Wants me to prove I love him by having sex.
C Doesn't really care about my feelings and puts me down.
D Is someone I've just met.

A Laughing and understanding are important when you think of having first-time sex with someone. You need to be safe in your heart and your body. Communication is everything. The first time is going to have a few moments where you need to laugh.
B If someone is asking you to 'prove your love' by having sex with them, then they don't love you but are using a situation to their advantage. Sex pressure is not okay and it's abusive.
C Someone who puts you down and doesn't respect your feelings does not deserve to have you around them. You are wasting your time on someone who uses you to vent their bad feelings. Spend time with your friends, talk to someone you trust and enjoy your freedom without the pressure of a bad relationship.

D If you've just met someone and feel like they 'could be it'—think carefully. Are you willing to share your first-time sex experience with someone who you may never see again? Before you do anything else, talk to them and try to work out who they are. 'Love at first sight' does not have to mean 'sex on the first date'.

3. IF I COULD SET A GIRL-RULE FOR FIRST-TIME SEX, IT WOULD BE:

A Condoms. I don't want to get pregnant or catch diseases.

B Stop! I might not be as ready as I thought.

C I can't set any rules! Otherwise he'll dump me.

D Affection first.

A Unprotected sex can lead to unplanned pregnancy and to STIs. Condoms and lubricant are the best protection against both, if used properly. You don't want to be starting your new exploration into sex and love with an infection or an unwanted pregnancy.

B If you start to have sex for the first time and want to stop, then say stop and expect it to stop. You can say stop for any reason or for no reason.

C If someone tries to force you by saying they will leave, then they are emotionally manipulating you. They don't care about you or your feelings. Move on and get support to help you. You deserve to be cared about and respected.

D Affection is one of the great joys of a healthy sex life. Touching, cuddles, strokes, kissing and sexual play are important for girls. Sex can always come later on if you want.

4. MY MAIN EMOTION WHEN THINKING ABOUT FIRST-TIME SEX IS:

A Excited—I know when it will be right and I'll be ready.

B Nervous—This is a little scary, I'll need a drink!

C Numb—I just want to get this over and done with.

D Scared—I don't know what to expect. Help!

A Your feelings can tell you how ready you are for first-time sex. Whatever feelings you have are normal. The important thing is what you do about those feelings.

B Suppressing your feelings with alcohol or drugs means you might not be doing something you really want to do and you're only doing it because someone else expects it.

C Denying your feelings definitely means you need to stop. Listen to yourself, think clearly and breathe. Think again.

D Being scared just means you need more time and should wait until you feel ready.

5. THE PERSON I HAVE FIRST-TIME SEX WITH WILL BE SOMEONE WHO:

A I can trust to respect my body and my wishes.

B Will adore me whether we have sex or not.

C Has a hot body and gorgeous eyes.

D Has the best come-on line.

A and **B** First-time sex has a lot to do with who you are with. So expect to be respected and to be totally, unconditionally adored—whether you have sex with them or you don't.

C Sure, you need to feel physically attracted to the other person. But you also need the respect and emotional understanding central to what you do and where you take it.

D Cheesy one-liners come from people who don't know you. They're also not very original and you can change the direction of this encounter easily. Ask them their full name, drivers licence number, marital status and number of children they have. Or ignore them. You might be surprised. Don't fall for them. Stay smart and in control.

'CAN I SAY WHAT I WANT AND BE STRONG AT THE SAME TIME?'

A good relationship . . . and great sex

You may not be able to see into the future but you can get early signs of whether this person is 'the one' for you. Commitment is when you choose to be with one other person because you love them, with all the ups and downs that come with that, and you behave in a way that reinforces the relationship as your main focus.

We choose to love someone because we know them, accept them for who they are and want them in our life. Loving someone is also about accepting the things that we may not always desire! They may not always be our friends' idea of the perfect guy; they might look different, wear the wrong clothes, laugh in a weird way or just not be trendy or cool. With real love, that doesn't matter. Developing trust and openness can be hard, but this is an important part of sharing love. When you love someone, it means you want them to be at least as happy as you are. It means genuinely caring for each other and will happen when you are ready to have a long-term relationship.

Tough call? Commitment can be a serious business. But it also includes friendship, fun, play and exploration. In fact, the good stuff can get even better with someone you want to be with for the long term.

Commitment requires certain qualities, like:

Responsibility—being adult in yourself and in the relationship
Tolerance—putting up with the things that don't fit with you
Patience—being calm when you have to wait or be supportive
Care—looking after someone who needs you emotionally and physically
Vision—knowing this is for the long term and working towards that.

They are NOT 'the one' when:

- You feel put down.
- They do not respect the important people in your life.
- They don't let you see your friends.
- You're not sharing quality time.
- It's only 'just for fun'.
- It 'doesn't mean anything'.
- Either of you keeps important information from the other.
- Either of you is pursuing other people—flirtatiously or otherwise.
- Either of you is having a sexual encounter outside of the relationship.
- Either of you wants a relationship 'break'.
- Either of you threatens to call it all off.
- Either of you keeps it a secret from other people over time.

You may want a relationship or you may just want to have sex, for sex, for now. You are a sexual being with sexual rights and responsibilities. You might care for and like someone but it doesn't always have to end up in marriage. But it has to be respectful whatever it is. It's your right to have someone honour you for who you are.

'WHAT DOES LOVE MEAN TO ME IN A RELATIONSHIP?'

TRICKY QUESTIONS

Q **How can I tell if someone is 'right' for me?**

A If you've met someone who sets off your 'feel good' vibe, here's a little checklist to see how okay they really are for you:

- Are they genuinely nice to you?
- Are they respectful to girls generally and you specifically?
- Are they not a show-off to get attention?
- Do they have plans for their own life?
- Do they like your friends, or at least respect your relationship with them?
- Do they show up when they say and do what they agree to do?
- Do they respect you and don't blab to their friends about the private things you do together?
- Do you both have physical attraction?
- Do you feel happy and secure?
- Can you both be loving and playful with each other?
- Do you want to spend enough time together?
- Do you enjoy each other's friends and respect personal space?

The good news is that we can be open to meet people who can be perfect in their own unique, individual way. That's why other people come into our lives—to sometimes show us new and different things, and hopefully better ways of living life and looking at the world.

Q I've fallen for my friend's boyfriend. He also looks at me 'that' way and says things that suggest he is 'interested'. What do I do?

A Think very carefully before you go with someone else's boyfriend. Often relationships that start from deception and secrecy end in tears. Having a 'crush' on someone else's boyfriend is fine if you don't act on it—you'll get over it soon. Infidelity hurts people, and not just the friend left behind.

Your relationship with your friend is important. You don't have to tell her your feelings, and you don't have to tell her that her boyfriend is giving you 'vibes' unless you think he's doing stuff that's going to hurt her. Ask yourself: Would you want to be in the shoes of your friend? Would you want to be with a guy who flirts with your friends? You wouldn't. So maybe this guy isn't quite as good as you think. Loyalty, trust, respect—they're the important things in *any* relationship including your friend's.

Q If a guy is hard and aroused then I have to have sex with him, don't I? Otherwise he will get 'blue balls' and hurt like crazy.

A 'Blue balls' is a term some guys use to describe the sensation of having an erection without ejaculation. The state of a guy's penis or testicles upon erection is his responsibility, not yours. You don't have to do anything you don't want to given that his physical reaction is not your responsibility. That includes having sex or continuing to have sex if you've started but don't want to continue.

'WHAT ARE MY DEEP VALUES FOR A RELATIONSHIP, THE VALUES I WON'T BUDGE ON?'

Chapter 5

Doing It

'I want the ins and outs of sex—
how to do it and make the most of it.'

'We want to know about different positions, how to have good sex and great sex, how to get the best from sex ourselves and not just how to make our boyfriend feel good.'

Girls, here it is, the chapter about sex, about doing it. The stuff we talked about earlier was the basic info: your body bits, feelings, pleasure and, very importantly, your being yourself. This is all stuff you need to know before you start checking out sex for real to help you make the choices that are right for you. If you've read this far and felt like it was a little too much information then I'd suggest you take this section in stages and only read certain parts when you feel you are ready.

Kissing

Kissing is one way to check out the chemistry between you and a sexual partner to see if you match. But a kiss is not just a kiss. A kiss between lovers can say 'I care about you'. A French kiss can say 'I want you, babe'. Or a kiss on the cheek can say 'Hello' or 'Goodbye'. So kissing says a lot.

HOW TO MAKE YOUR KISSES GOOD

Don't stress. Just relax, breathe (otherwise you'll have a dizzy spell and pass out) and focus on gentle lip touching, smelling and eye gazing—as a starter. Turn your head but don't twist your neck (ouch!).

Holding back a little at the beginning provides great build-up and excitement, keeps you in control and keeps your boyfriend wanting more! You are a girl, not a sports car. If too much is happening too soon, then say so. Stop, have a break, say you need to stop, go to the loo, whatever. You can talk during a kiss-fest—if you want to and need to. You can also take it a step further and touch your boyfriend while kissing—this means that things are getting hotter.

Remember though:

- Kissing someone with bad breath is a turn-off, so brush your teeth (don't miss your tongue), keep a mint handy and keep yourself healthy.
- Watch those teeth—clashing incisors could possibly be fun when things get rowdy (like in mating rituals of wild animals) but it could also hurt! Nibbling gently, however, is exciting.
- Watch your saliva—slobbering is so unsexy.
- 'Tonguing' doesn't mean sticking it in another person's mouth or throat without a decent lead-up—take it easy and build up to it gently, provocatively and lovingly.
- Hickeys (bruises, usually on a neck caused by sucking) are ugly so keep them at bay.

Kissing your partner does not mean you have to have sex with them. Know how far you want to go. Check in with yourself, the part of you that is sussing out the situation regardless of the hormones pumping through you.

TYPES OF KISSES

PECK ON THE CHEEK greeting

TWO PECKS, ONE ON EACH CHEEK greeting in some cultures (for example, Italian)

FRENCH KISSING not actually French and not a greeting, but using tongue in mouth while kissing (sounds yewh, but it might feel actually okay if it's turning you on)

BRIEF LIP KISSING greeting between good friends, only for special people

LONG LIP KISSING sharing a sexual or emotional moment with your special someone

Butterfly kissing eyelashes on cheeks (cute!)

AIR KISSING the 'mwah, mwah' used by aspiring movie stars where the lips never meet the surface of your skin, cheek or otherwise—for fun with your girl friends

BLOWING KISSES kissing your palm and blowing in someone's direction (fun and flirty)

HAND KISSING kissing top of hand (smarmy or cute depending on who's doing it)

YUCK KISSES if a kiss leaves you feeling like you've been mauled or slobbered on, or like you've been kissing a plank, or like you will choke on a tongue and it's not yours, then you probably won't be lining up for more with that person

DID YOU KNOW?

Not all cultures have kissing as a greeting. The Maori in New Zealand touch noses, the Inuit in North America rub noses. Kissing and rubbing noses have the same intention of smelling the person. In some cultures, kissing in public is not acceptable public behaviour.

Kissing requires at least 20 muscles working together.

Kissing also features in children's fairytales. Remember Sleeping Beauty and the Frog Prince? Some primates also use kissing as a form of social bonding.

Sex or great sex?

There is sex . . . and there is great sex. So, what's the difference?

Having sex can be just about 'doing it'. But who wants that? It can take some practice to have sex that you feel fantastic about. It also takes getting to know your body and feeling comfortable in your skin. Libido, or sex drive, has a lot to do with how much people enjoy sex. So does feeling safe and being able to choose whether you have sex and how.

Having sex with a new person can feel exciting simply because it's new, not necessarily because it's good. Having great sex is not about having more partners than anyone else—that's just a competition. But having sex with someone who means something to you can make it mind-blowing. Knowing you are special to someone else is important and means you are worth every drop of sexual energy you share with them.

Great sex is all about communication. Don't assume they always know or want what is good for you. Be honest and up-front about what you want and don't want. You should always be able to say how you feel. If you feel happy, scared, safe, painful or great, you need to be able to say so. If you can't, then this might be a sign to say that this person may not be the right one for you or that you may not be as ready for sexual activity as you thought.

Now this might sound weird but great sex is not just about a penis. Both guys and girls are often compelled into thinking that great sex revolves around a guy's penis and what a girl or guy does with it. Music video clips, magazines and advertising revolve around that stuff. So it seems like great sex is penis-focused, right?

Wrong!

Remember, there's a whole person connected to that penis. Great sex is about enjoying someone else's mind and body, not just their private parts!

The main rule for girls and great sex is—slow, steady, gentle, consistent.

The rule for guys from girls is—trust, safe, fun, exploration and a little conversation!

Condoms and lube can and should always be a part of your great sex plan. Yes, they can make sex fun and, let's face it, they will generally be the one thing you will be grateful for always using. Lube makes sex more comfortable and keeps condoms on. Condoms will keep most STIs (sexually transmissible infections—we will talk about this later in the book) at bay and are one of your best resources in reducing the chances of having an unplanned pregnancy. Remember never to leave this little best friend at home and ruin an otherwise potentially great sexual experience.

Negotiating condom use is one skill you will never ever regret practising. Part of your assessment as to whether he is worth having sex with is his attitude to using condoms. If he offers his own condoms then he is on the right track. If he doesn't, then you can suggest something like: 'I think this might go further and I want to use condoms if it does. I presume that will be all right with you?' If he says something very disappointing to indicate his unwillingness, then you are able to say something like: 'I'm committed to using condoms. We either have safe sex or no sex.' There are more good reasons to use condoms than not to use them, apart from not having sex. There are no genuine alternatives to good condom use. Remember, this is your body we are talking about here. There will be more information on condoms later in the book.

'HOW CAN I FEEL MORE COMFORTABLE WITH CONDOMS? AND HOW CAN I SAY WHAT I NEED REGARDING CONDOM USE?'

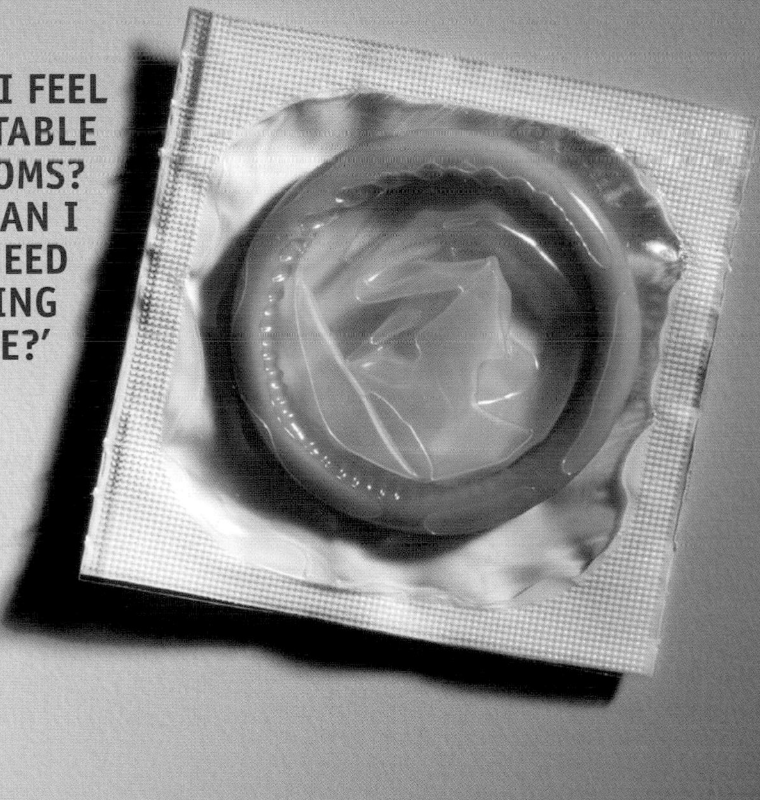

FOREPLAY

Girls need foreplay. And, for many girls, foreplay *is* sex. Foreplay is sexual activity that does not involve actually having sexual intercourse (vagina over the penis sex). Communication, laughing, playing, tickling, cuddling and stroking are all foreplay. Kissing and fondling are classic foreplay.

Fondling and playing with nipples can be sexy for both guys and girls as the nipples are a very sensitive erogenous zone. You might also find having your nipples stroked, sucked or licked very erotic. During foreplay the areas of your body and your boyfriend's body worth touching are soft skin areas such as neck, wrist, elbow, inner thigh or back of knees. Wetness makes this type of foreplay fun and less irritating on skin, so this is where your tongue can come in handy. Saliva is a natural lubricant and great for juicing up erogenous zones.

Foreplay can sometimes take longer than sexual intercourse. If you relax and give it time, you will enjoy it so much more and stay in touch with your body. If you are ready and want to go a little further, spending time on foreplay and stimulation of your clitoris without penetration is often the best way for a girl to orgasm. Foreplay also builds trust and effectively sifts out the boys who are happy to do foreplay with a girl from the boys who are too rushed and penis-centric.

DRY SEX

Dry sex, or 'frottage', is a kind of 'outercourse' or sex without penetration. It's when two people rub their bodies, usually their genitals, against each other, simulating sexual intercourse. It can be exciting and can lead to orgasm. Dry sex often happens when you are partly or fully clothed, so it's a good option for people not ready to have sex naked. It's also safer in terms of STIs because no body fluids are exchanged unless there is skin-to-skin genital contact or fluid exposure.

ORAL SEX

Oral sex has been around for centuries! It refers to using the mouth and tongue to sexually stimulate another person's genital area. For you, it means your boyfriend sucking or licking with the flat and pointy end of his tongue on and around your clitoris. It is often the most successful way for a woman to reach orgasm.

Your boyfriend needs to be patient and consistent, and in a comfy position—he could be there for a little while—but it shows that he wants to pleasure you. Give him feedback as he goes to tell him if he is on track or not. Communication is the key to satisfying both of you.

Your clitoris requires special attention and too much pressure can make it too sensitive, not enough and it's ho-hum. Remember slow, steady and wet. Your vulva is sensitive and stimulation can be very arousing, so direct your boyfriend to what feels good for you. But using his teeth is generally not a good idea.

Explore different positions—lying on your back, on your hands and knees, sitting in a chair, standing, straddling—the choice is only limited by your imagination and comfort levels. You do it because you want to and you know you are ready in yourself.

Oral sex won't lead to pregnancy, but oral sex is considered to be a kind of sexual intercourse. If you use your mouth for sexual stimulation of his penis you also need to use condoms to protect you from STIs, which can be transmitted from the genitals to the lips, mouth and throat, and from mouth to genitals. You also do not have to 'swallow' his semen (cum) or have him orgasm into your mouth. If he is going to orgasm, then he can forewarn you so he can ejaculate outside of your mouth. You can agree to decide as you go and you can stop whenever you want.

Using water-based lubricant can really help to reduce friction and increase sensitivity. You can buy it from the supermarket or chemist. Some youth centres and sexual health clinics provide lubricant for free. You can use it for DIY (masturbation) or for sexual intercourse. See the boys' section for more on how to please them orally.

69

This is mutual oral sex in a 'top-to-toe' position, where two people can give each other oral stimulation with their mouths at the same time. Using your hands and fingers in this position can be great for giving mutual masturbation at the same time, too. Sometimes you might need to stop 'giving' if you need to be focused on your own body for a while, particularly if you feel close to orgasm. Stay in tune with yourself and feel what it wants and doesn't want each moment.

MUTUAL MASTURBATION

Touching, fondling and stroking each other's genitals can be highly arousing and enjoyable. Apart from self-masturbation, it's probably the safest form of sex—as long as semen does not go in or near your vagina. Mutual masturbation can take practice to work out what you each enjoy—it's different for everyone. You might be sitting next to each other, on top of your partner or standing, or have them kneeling while you lie down. The basic rule is to use lots of lube or saliva to keep any friction in check.

You could ask your partner to slowly, gently and consistently fondle and stroke your vulva. If you wish, they can insert a finger or two into your vagina and press at the front, top side, where your G-spot is—this can be very erotic. Having your clitoris stimulated gently and steadily with lots of lube is very exciting and the way many women reach orgasm.

Remember, if you are not enjoying this or don't feel comfortable, then stop.

PENETRATIVE VAGINAL SEX

This is when, with mutual consent (you both want to), a guy's penis is inserted into a girl's vagina and, with a rocking motion, it is moved in and out. It can also involve penetration with consent of a finger or sex toy. A girl can also straddle on top and insert the penis herself using her body. It creates an exciting friction for a guy's penis, and stimulates a girl's vagina and sometimes her clitoris. A woman's vulva can be very sensitive prior to a penis entering it, particularly after foreplay, so this can be very exciting.

Although the vagina does not have many nerve endings, the position you are in during intercourse can make a difference to your sexual pleasure. You can be on top or lying down or whatever feels good for you. Go slowly and try different positions. If it hurts, stop and ask your boyfriend to withdraw his penis or move your body. Listen to your body and say what you want.

Having sex has a lot to do with feeling safe and being sexually attracted to the other person. Doing it just for the other person's benefit is not a good reason to have sex, and it can really make sex painful and you unhappy and pressured. Fear of getting pregnant and of intercourse itself can make a girl's vagina dry and tight. Nervousness about getting caught is another factor that can make a girl feel uncomfortable.

If you are having sex when you don't really want to, or if you're not ready, this can contribute to feeling numb in your body (your mind trying to shut it out) or feeling pain. Your muscles tense up and your body is not ready for it, making the vaginal muscles clamp together as a reflex reaction. Sometimes pain comes from not being aroused and having no lubricant as having a dry vagina can make intercourse very painful.

Communication is the key. You can expect your partner to ask you how you are feeling. You can also tell them if you are feeling okay or whether you are not liking this experience. If it is hurting, or if you are not comfortable, you can stop and take a rest. You might want to try again, but you do not have to continue then if you don't want to. This is where communication, feeling safe and being cared about really counts. You might want to move, kiss, laugh or just be held. This is a moment when you need to choose what is okay for you at the time. It's important that you feel safe and communicate what you want. Ask him to go slow or stop when you want him to. Use lube on the outside of the condom. Try a position where you are comfortable, and be in a place where you feel safe and will not be interrupted. If you've tried all these things and you still feel pain, maybe you need to give yourself a break. Maybe you are not ready to have sex yet. Maybe you need to give it some time. Be patient and kind with yourself, stay strong and don't fall for sexual pressure.

'DOES SEX HURT THE FIRST TIME?'

ANAL SEX

Anal sex usually involves using a finger, mouth, penis or sex toy to stimulate the delicate nerve endings in, and penetrate, the anus. It is a form of sexual intercourse, although you cannot become pregnant from it. Like any sexual activity, you only engage in anal sex if you want to. It may not be for everyone and it's okay to not want to have anal sex. With practice some girls enjoy anal sex, although many girls do find that anal sex can hurt. The anus is lined with delicate skin and can easily tear and bleed with any friction.

If you choose to have anal sex, it is vitally important to use a condom and plenty of lubricant—every time. Anal sex is one way HIV, STIs and other infections can enter your body, as the anal skin tissue is thin and small injuries can occur without you realising it. As a precaution, do not allow something that has been in your anus to enter your vagina as this can cause infections; so change condoms.

Always go slowly with anal sex. Enjoying anal sex can take practice, communication and trust. As with any sexual activity if it hurts at any point, stop.

'HOW DO I FEEL RIGHT NOW?'

Sex and gender relationships

FRIENDS WITH BENEFITS

Having sex with a friend, or friends 'with benefits' as it is commonly known, can be an experience that some girls say just kind of happens, with no emotional ties, no baggage, no commitment, no talk of relationship and no future stuff. Girls can, and do, have sex for . . . sex.

Sex with a friend might seem like an option if you've agreed you're both not ready for a relationship but you're ready for sexual exploration. It might also seem safer to have sex with a friend than with someone you have just met at a dance club. If all this sounds familiar, there are some things you need to be aware of. If you're exploring sex with a friend because you want to, because you want to try things out, then be honest and safe with each other also. Remember you were friends first. Just keep in mind that having sex just to make someone your boyfriend isn't a great idea. That might turn out to be a sad and unhappy experience in the long run. There's a fine line between exploring sex and being exploited.

While having sex with a friend might be a temporary arrangement, your whole life is spent with you. So stay cool, stay in touch, be yourself. Take care of your body and always protect yourself and use a condom. This may not become a committed relationship so expect the friend also to have sex with other people. Your friend should also not expect you to be committed to them only, unless you both discuss and agree to be monogamous. If they are a lot older than you, that could be a problem. Think about the 'creep factor', when older guys want to have sex with much younger girls. Remember there might be laws about this where you live.

And consider too that sex often changes relationships. Think about what might happen after the sex. What happens if one of you wants a relationship? How would you feel if they wanted to be with you exclusively? What if you want more? Are you exploring sex or really substituting sex for affection?

Your sexual activity doesn't need to be a news flash to your other friends. Talk about it to someone you trust if you need advice and support, or if it is abusive or you're scared. You need to know you can share this news with mutual respect. Be really clear that within your 'with benefits' arrangement neither of you is controlling the other. Is there respect between you both? Could you call it off at any point and still be friends?

SEXUAL DIVERSITY AND SAME-SEX ATTRACTION

Human beings are amazingly complex and diverse. We not only explore our sexual expression and choices in this book, but we also truly celebrate the wonderful diversity that our sexual, emotional and love lives can express. Not all things can be classified, although for simplicity, we will try to clarify them here. Sexuality is usually described in three ways: heterosexual (straight), homosexual (gay or lesbian), or bisexual (bi) and might be how a person experiences their romantic and sexual attraction to someone of the same or opposite biological sex. A person who identifies as heterosexual is predominantly attracted to someone of the opposite biological sex, a person identifying as homosexual is predominantly attracted to someone of the same sex and a person who is bisexual is attracted, on the whole, to both biological sexes. A person can also identify as asexual which means they are generally attracted to neither sex.

Although someone might identify with one sexual identity, this can be relatively fluid. For example, someone who identifies as heterosexual may have a genuine romantic attraction in their lifetime to someone of the same gender. This may not mean that they identify as homosexual or bisexual. What tends to define our sexual orientation is our behaviour, inclinations, desires and sense of social belonging. Some people may be oriented as homosexual but their behaviour and identity may be as a married heterosexual. This can be very confusing for them and they may find it difficult to accept their own genuine sense of sexual self. Some societies have been persecutory of people who have not identified as heterosexual and, although thankfully this is changing, it has contributed to a lot of pain and difficulty for many people.

Sexual orientation is like eye colour. Sometimes you might try to mask it if you've been told it's wrong or bad but you cannot change it. And why should you? It's a normal wonderful part of who you are. It can sometimes be confusing to work out your own sexual preferences as you grow up, given that much of the world might appear to be heterosexual. It can feel pretty lonely when no one else owns up to having the same kind of feelings and longings as you. Everyone wants to fit in.

Working out your own sexual orientation is a part of your teenage years. Some people just know by the time they are eight years old that they just don't conform to a strictly heterosexual path, and have attempted to work it out from there. Who would think of changing a heterosexual person from their sexual orientation? It's no more possible or desirable to change a homosexual person into a straight one. It's true that some people think homosexuality is a 'problem' that needs to be fixed. But we now know that attitude is 'homophobia' or the fear of homosexuality—and those people are the ones who need help!

Girls have sex with girls for a variety of reasons. Some girls experiment with their sexual identity and with their own sexual power. They may or may not identify as a lesbian although they may be same-sex attracted. (Being same-sex attracted means a person feels sexually attracted to someone of the same sex.) If a girl is same-sex attracted, then she may want to be sexual with another girl rather than a guy. There are many variations in nature, and this also applies to human sexuality.

In Australia, same-sex relationships are legal and a homosexual person generally has the same rights and responsibilities regarding sex as a heterosexual person. There are variations across each state regarding age of consent. People who are same-sex attracted or homosexual do have children, careers, friends, parents that love and are proud of them, and relationships. In other words, your sexual orientation—regardless of whether it's same sex, opposite sex, both or neither—should be a natural part of having a normal, healthy, productive and successful life.

'WHEN I THINK OF BEING ATTRACTED TO SOMEONE, WHAT DOES THAT FEEL LIKE AND LOOK LIKE TO ME?'

SEX STUFF AND GENDER STUFF

Sex and gender are different but connected parts of ourselves. Our gender is defined by:

- the world we live in
- the body we were born in
- the feelings that we have inside.

When someone asks what 'sex' a baby is when they are born, this refers to their body parts, such as penis and testicles for boys and vaginas and ovaries for girls. This relates to the kinds of dominant sex hormones produced to create sex characteristics. Gender, however, is different: it refers to the gender roles like 'masculine' or 'feminine'. Gender also refers to how we might feel about ourselves—our gender identity as a man or woman.

Sometimes, how someone feels about their own self doesn't match how others perceive them, or how their body displays their 'sex'. Their feelings about their gender identity may also not match what their body says about them. Transgender is a general term referring to people whose gender identity or presentation does not fit traditional norms. It occurs across cultures and is more common than you'd think. It is different to playing or pretending to experience another gender through cross-dressing (guys wearing women's clothing, for example), which can be fun but does not make a person transgender.

'Gender identity dysphoria' is the medical term that identifies when a person's sense of gender identity is not matched by their physical characteristics, and this can cause them social and personal distress. How they feel does not match the body they are in. Transgender can occur either male-to-female or female-to-male. Intersex is a physical condition when a person's sexual organs are not obviously male or female when they are born or their sex doesn't match their physiological make-up. For example, a person may have male genitals and look male but will have XX (female) chromosomes. Sometimes they are born with genitals that do not conform to what society thinks is normal. They may have a penis that is smaller than average, or a clitoris that is larger than average. When a baby is born with indiscriminate genitalia, the hospital and parents make a decision on the gender of the child until they can talk and consult with them. As a result some mistakes are made about what a child's actual gender identity really is. This can create a lot of confusion for teenagers who are beginning to discover and explore their own sexual and gender identity—teenagers who need unconditional support to assist them to work out their life trajectory. Our society needs to do more to understand and accept that people do not always come in simple categories of male and female. Support, acceptance and celebration of the natural diversity of gender and sexual identity is actually part of the normal everyday wonderful world we live in.

TRICKY QUESTIONS

Q I don't feel attracted to either guys or girls. Am I weird?

A Sexual attraction can mean different things to different people. Generally, a person who does not feel sexually attracted to other people may call themselves 'asexual'. Usually, people who define themselves as asexual are quite content and comfortable with this definition. Being asexual is not a disease or a health problem. People who are uninterested in sex do not necessarily have sexual identity issues. They generally know if they are gay, straight, bi, etc.—it's the acts of sex they are not interested in, not their sexual identity. Sometimes, a person is asexual only for a part of their life, such as after the break-up of a relationship; sometimes they are asexual for life. You may not be attracted to the right person now but that might change over time, or it might not. You might want to talk to someone you trust about it if this feels unhealthy or is worrying you.

Q What does it mean to 'lose your virginity'?

A This is indeed a tricky question as much depends on what you believe virginity to be. Technically it means you have had sexual intercourse or have consented to sexual activity, which could include penis-in-vagina sex, oral sex, anal sex, or having someone else's finger inserted into the vagina or anus through consensual sexual activity. In some cultures, loss of virginity means a girl's hymen has been 'broken'. A hymen that is not intact (covering the vagina) is seen (inaccurately) as 'proof' that a girl has had sexual intercourse. However, the hymen usually has a natural hole in it and a hymen rarely completely covers the vagina for many virgin girls. If a girl is menstruating and her hymen is covering the vagina, then she will need to see a doctor who can help her body release the menstrual fluid.

Q Does sex hurt the first time?

A A lot of girls worry about whether their first experience of sexual intercourse will hurt and if they will bleed as a result of tearing. Having first-time sex does use parts of your body which have never had so much physical and emotional focus. If you feel anxious or nervous before your first time, this tension can make your vagina dry and the vaginal muscles may clench tightly, which can be very uncomfortable and might cause pain. Feeling sexually turned on is important as it allows vaginal fluid to line the vagina and the muscles to relax and open up for intercourse. Using your fingers around the vagina and clitoris can help lubricate and relax your vagina. You might think about practising touching yourself with your fingers around your vagina and genitals when you are having a bath or lying down somewhere private. You can even try inserting a finger into your vagina to explore and see how that feels. You might even try to see if you can touch your cervix. (The distance between your vaginal entrance and your cervix is about the length of your middle finger.) This helps you get used to the feeling of something else coming into your vagina at your pace and in your safe space. Using water-based lubricant is really helpful, whether you are exploring by yourself or with your partner.

A few girls report having some bleeding when they first have sex. It may be caused by the stretching of the soft skin in the vagina. The vaginal muscles are quite strong but the tissue and membranes can be delicate and small tears can occur with repeated friction. Having condoms and lube is essential. Condoms will reduce the chance of sexually transmissible infections being transmitted and lube helps with moisture and reduces friction which can cause bleeding.

'WHEN I THINK OF HAVING SEX THE FIRST TIME, WHAT FEELINGS AND THOUGHTS COME UP?'

Q **What if all my friends have had sex except me?**

A The likelihood that all your friends have actually had sex is probably not as high as you might think. In Australia, the majority of young people in senior high school (aged 16 to 18 years) are sexually active in some way. This includes a whole range of sexual activity such as kissing, genital touching and oral sex. However, about 50 per cent of young adults 16 to 18 years of age report having had sexual intercourse. So only about half have had some kind of intercourse—not everybody, and most likely not all of your friends. Sometimes people are misinformed about sex and may not know all the facts. Some people also might think that talking about having sex makes them more acceptable. It's okay. They'll get over it. Peer pressure can be one of the biggest stresses in a girl's life. Sometimes the idea that you're missing out can be the biggest stress of all. The most important thing to remember is that you will have sex when you are ready, and not when you are pressured. After all, if and when you finally go there—because you really want to—you will be thinking of 'other things' and not your friends.

Q What is abstinence?

A The definition of abstinence varies. It can apply to the avoidance of sexual intercourse (oral, anal or vaginal). Or it can also apply to the avoidance of any sexual activity. Some people practise abstinence as a way of avoiding pregnancy or transmission of sexually transmissible infections, or for religious or cultural reasons. People who practise abstinence may have clear sexual drives and sexual identity but they choose not to engage in sexual activity. Sexual abstinence is a personal choice. You must feel comfortable and happy to abstain for as long as you choose, and how you define it is up to you.

Q Is having sex during your period weird?

A No. Sex during your period is quite normal. In fact, many girls can feel sexually aroused around the time of their period. Some people like having sex during their period and some people don't. It just takes negotiation. It also means checking out ways to manage the blood. You can still become pregnant during this time; there's no sure way of knowing when that egg will be released; and you can still catch STIs if you have unprotected sex during your period. So all the precautions apply.

Q Fanny farts make sex embarrassing. Why does this happen?

A It's really normal and very common, although a bit embarrassing. When your body is sexually aroused, the vagina pulls up and back, creating a vacuum effect by sucking in air. When the vagina returns to its normal position, it releases the air, making a farting sound. It's hard to avoid, but laughing about it yourself takes the tension out of the situation and makes it easier to discuss. Just affirm that it's normal for any girl.

Q Is sex the price you pay to keep a relationship?

A If sex feels like 'a price to pay' then it's more expensive than what your partner is worth. Find someone who wants you for you, not just for sex. Sex is meant to be shared and you have a right to a happy sexual life, as well as a loving relationship. It's not a trade-off. In the end, if the relationship is just based on you 'putting out', then it won't really work and the other person won't stay.

Chapter 6

Safer Sex

'There were a few pregnancy scares at school. You hear stories. Girls get scared. You can't deal with having a baby at 17.'

'A friend of mine was crying because she found out she had [an STI]. She was so angry to have one so early in her life. You know, it rocked all of us.'

We've talked a lot about sex being fun and, like most fun things, there are a few risks involved. We need to talk about some of the things you might need to consider avoiding if you want to continue having a fabulous and healthy love life well into the future. Contraception is something that every girl needs to think about if she wants to start having sex and doesn't want to get pregnant. STIs (sexually transmissible infections) are a very real part of sex, and you need to know about them.

The facts about contraception

Pregnancy can occur from the very first time two people have sex. Yep, it just takes one very ripe egg, one very eager sperm and one sexual encounter. Whether you want to be pregnant is not the issue for those little numbers! Using contraception means choosing to take control over your reproductive potential. Choosing to not become pregnant is a wise, clever and smart decision when you are not ready to be a mother.

There is no completely 100 per cent foolproof method of contraception. The only sexual activity that comes with a pregnancy-free guarantee is masturbation. All contraception has a failure rate, although if used properly, this is generally low. So despite the best planning and decision making in the world, a girl can become pregnant if she has sex.

There are different kinds of contraception for different girls. Some do have side-effects and shouldn't be used if you have certain health conditions. You should consult a doctor you trust, or go to a family planning clinic for advice. Remember, you are totally entitled to see a clinician about contraception, one who does not judge you in any way, who will give you the right advice, and won't limit your options according to their values.

This is only a brief overview of contraceptive options. You can check out a stack of websites for more details. We've included a few websites we like for you to search in the 'Learning More' section. Use your own judgement. Keep looking and get informed.

THE CONDOM

The condom is a sheath made of latex or polyurethane that is put on the penis to stop semen entering your vagina. It creates a barrier. When used properly with water-based lubricant (lots of fun!), it has 95 to 98 per cent success rate for avoiding pregnancy and STI transmission—which is pretty good value for a cheap bit of rubber.

Condoms can be purchased in supermarkets and pharmacies and are also available from youth health centres and family planning clinics—for free! To use a condom, put it on the penis when it is hard and before it enters your vagina. Apply lubricant. When the guy ejaculates (cums) he needs to take his penis out pretty soon afterwards. Otherwise his penis will shrink and semen will go everywhere, including into your vagina. Always check the condom's expiry date and the instructions. Throw away in the bin, not the loo.

THE ORAL CONTRACEPTIVE PILL (OCP)

The OCP or oral contraceptive pill is a hormonal contraceptive taken in tablet form every day by a woman. It is designed to prevent you from ovulating and it changes the lining of your uterus. It can be very effective when taken regularly, and there are plenty of choices about types, brands and their effects. You'll need a prescription from your doctor for it. You cannot use someone else's pill. The advantage of the pill is that you can stop taking it easily and it will not cause infertility. But it does not offer STI protection.

THE EMERGENCY PILL (OR MORNING-AFTER PILL)

The emergency pill is just that, for emergency use only, after unprotected sex or if the condom breaks or falls off. It works firstly by delaying ovulation, and secondly by discouraging implantation of a fertilised ovum. It comes as a set of pills and is made up of contraceptive hormones, but you must take it as soon as possible after unprotected sex. The longer you leave it, the less effect it has on preventing pregnancy. You can take the emergency pill up to five days after unprotected sex. You can take it more than once in a menstrual cycle and it is available over the counter at your pharmacy (the pharmacist will need to ask a few questions first) or through doctors or family planning clinics. Follow the instructions. Like OCPs, it does not offer any STI protection.

WITHDRAWAL METHOD

The withdrawal method is when the penis (without condom) is withdrawn from your vagina before ejaculation. You should only use this method when a guy knows his body really, really, really, really well. But the fact is it's not that reliable as a contraceptive, no matter what he says, nor is it protective from STIs.

It's free, but there might be a hefty cost down the track with an unplanned pregnancy or an STI, and you will need a towel to clean up afterwards! Talk to a doctor you trust about this as an option, but it is not recommended.

DIAPHRAGMS

A diaphragm is a rubber 'cup' inserted by you into the vagina and placed over the cervix. It's a barrier method. You can insert it anytime before sex and leave it in for at least six hours after intercourse, then take it out and wash it—easy! It's fairly reliable as long as your weight doesn't fluctuate too much as the cup size needs to be right for you, and you need to know how it fits inside you. It is painless when inserting, but it requires familiarity with your vagina and cervix.

The initial cost can be a bit expensive but a diaphragm can last for ages. You can get fitted and purchase one at your doctor's or family planning clinic, and then practise putting it on. It offers little STI protection.

IUD (INTRAUTERINE DEVICE)

An IUD is a small instrument which is inserted into your uterus by a doctor using local anaesthetic. It confuses, and is toxic to, sperm. It can also prevent a successful implantation of the fertilised egg into the lining of your uterus. It is a very effective contraception method, up to 98 per cent against pregnancy, and can be removed in a clinic by a doctor. It is often used by women who have had kids.

It can be expensive initially but lasts for ages. There's also a hormonal version which can last for up to five years. You will need to talk to a doctor or family planning clinician first to see if this is right for you. It offers no STI protection.

DEPO, DMPA (DEPO METROXYPROGESTERONE ACETATE)

Depo is a hormonal injection that a doctor or nurse administers every three months. It's extremely effective against pregnancy—about 99 per cent. It prevents ovulation and is sometimes used for women who have menstrual problems. It offers no STI protection.

NATURAL FAMILY PLANNING

There are a number of natural methods available. All of them rely on you being extremely good at reading and documenting your body signs, a regular cycle, some periods of abstinence, lots of practice (and risk of failure), and sifting through other body signs such as tiredness and illness. Over time and with practice, you can get good at doing this and the method becomes a little more reliable. It is not recommended for young women because your periods and ovulation are normally too inconsistent to work out 'safe' times. It offers no protection against STIs.

'DO I KNOW WHERE TO GET CONTRACEPTION AND ADVICE?'

VAGINAL RING

This flexible rubber ring is made with hormones and is inserted into the vagina. The hormones move through the lining of the vagina into the bloodstream. You use a new one each month. It can be as effective as the pill if used properly, and has similar side-effects. It is available from doctors and family planning clinics. It offers no STI protection.

SPERMICIDE

This is meant to kill sperm in the vagina after sex. It is unreliable and is not recommended as a form of contraception on its own. It offers no STI protection.

CONTRACEPTIVE IMPLANT

This is a little flexible plastic rod inserted into your arm under the skin by a doctor in a clinic and lasts for up to three years. It releases hormones to prevent pregnancy. Like all hormonal contraceptive options, it may produce some side-effects which you can ask about with your doctor. It is very effective in preventing pregnancy. Does not protect you from STIs.

MYTHS ABOUT PREGNANCY

You won't get pregnant if you go to the toilet after sex.

You won't get pregnant if it's your first time.

You won't get pregnant if you haven't had your period yet.

You won't get pregnant if you have sex during your period.

You won't get pregnant if you have sex in the bath.

You won't get pregnant if you have sex standing up.

You won't get pregnant if you jump up and down after sex.

You won't get pregnant if you flush out your vagina with water/cola/vinegar.

You won't get pregnant if you squeeze your pelvic floor muscles to push the semen out.

You won't get pregnant if you have a bath or shower straight after sex.

The reality is, all of these myths are FALSE! The bottom line is that if you decide to have sex, then the only way to try to reduce the chance of pregnancy is to use contraception.

I think I'm pregnant!

If you have unprotected sex, then you can become pregnant. Some symptoms of pregnancy are a missed period, tender breasts, needing to urinate more often, nausea, feeling tired, and light-headedness. Some of these symptoms can also be caused by stress, not eating properly and too much exercise. If you have either no period or a light period or spotting and other symptoms, and you've had sex since your last period, then you might be pregnant.

What should you do? First of all, try to avoid the temptation of pretending it will go away. It is important that you make some decisions for yourself and *act* now. You can take emergency contraception in the first five days after unprotected sex. You can get a pregnancy test from a family planning or sexual health clinic, or a doctor or nurse (preferably one you feel comfortable with). A doctor can do a blood test to detect the presence of the pregnancy hormone five days after the time of conception. But it takes about 48 hours for the tests to be conducted at the lab and returned to the doctor. They can also do a urine test to check hormone levels that are present if you are pregnant. They are more accurate at the time that you would normally have your period. Home pregnancy tests can also be bought from pharmacies or supermarkets (see 'How does a home pregnancy test work?').

If you're not pregnant, that's not the end of the story. It's a good idea to get tests for STIs if you have had unprotected sex just to make sure you haven't picked up a bug (most can be treated). Talk to your doctor or a sexual health or family planning clinic. At the same time, talk to someone about a contraception that's best for you if you don't want to get pregnant.

If you're pregnant and didn't intend to be, it is likely that you might just want to hide and pretend it's not happening. Do not try to wish away, pretend or forget the pregnancy. You need to get some advice, so talk to someone about your feelings and your choices. Don't think you have to do this by yourself. Speak to a doctor you trust, family planning clinic, family member or supportive friend. The important thing is to have the right information and support to make the best decision for you. You have to look at the options, which be to:

» continue the pregnancy (which means raising, fostering or adopting the child)
» have a termination, i.e. an abortion (this is determined by a doctor. Just check out the laws in the state where you live).

You need to get information, counselling or referral options from a family planning clinic, youth centre or a doctor you trust. You have a right to have balanced information and support, whatever your decision. You can also contact agencies that specialise in this issue for advice, and look at web info to help you make informed choices (see 'Learning More' at the back of the book for further information).

HOW DOES A HOME PREGNANCY TEST WORK?

A pregnancy test is very simple, reliable and normally requires just a urine (pee) sample. Some tests require you to pee directly onto the strip while you are on the toilet and some require you to collect urine in a small container to allow the strip to soak in it for a short period of time (five minutes or so). Five minutes can feel like a long time, so have someone around for you to talk to, read a magazine or do something that relaxes you while you're waiting. The test is designed to pick up a change in hormones as a result of a pregnancy. If you're doing a home pregnancy test, you need to buy a twin pack. If your period does not show for a day or two but the first test is negative, it might mean that either you are not pregnant, or you are pregnant but the hormones are not high enough for the test to pick it up. Test again three days later just to make sure. Also check out 'Emergency contraception' in Chapter 5 of the boys' section of this book. Also, refer back to 'The emergency pill (or morning-after pill)' section of this book.

'WHO WOULD I TALK TO IF I WAS WORRIED I MIGHT BE PREGNANT?'

THE BIGGEST CHOICE

Babies can be extraordinarily cute and delightful. They can teach us a lot about patience and care, and they bring untold joy and satisfaction into their parents' lives. Most girls are brought up to expect to have a baby one day. We are led to believe that it is the fulfilment of womanhood and the best thing a woman can experience. We are not always told that having a baby is the single biggest change a woman can have in her life. There is nothing as *big* as having a baby.

Why? Because it's a commitment for the rest of your life. If you're thinking about having a baby, you have some very serious questions to ask yourself. But first, here are some facts you need to know:

- Being pregnant for 40 weeks means you have to look after your own health as a priority—no late nights, going out, partying, alcohol, cigarettes or drugs. You need to eat well, exercise and get plenty of rest. You might feel tired and sick, and you'll see your body changing dramatically. You will need check-ups and antenatal classes. Preparing to bring a baby into the world requires planning, resources and support.
- Giving birth can take anything from a few hours to a few days and requires pain management at the hospital and lots of physical and emotional support at the birth. You will be on a fast-track learning schedule.

- Caring for your baby means waking up and getting out of bed routinely during the night to soothe the crying baby. It means nappy changing, bathing, breastfeeding and bottle cleaning, and being extra careful physically and emotionally with a delicate little human all the time. The baby is now Number One. The baby rules your world.
- Parenting continues for the rest of your baby's life. Babies grow into toddlers, children, teenagers and adults—their presence in your world is permanent.

Are you ready for all that? It's not an easy road to go down for any woman and especially for teenagers. Ask yourself:

- Why do I want to have a baby? To be an adult and have respect from those around me? To get out of school? To do something different? To have someone to take care of?
- What do I want to do with my life in one year? Two years? Five years?
- Can I keep going to school if I have a baby? If I stop my education now, what will my future options and choices be?
- What other things do I want to do with my life: travel, develop my independence, meet lots of people, explore the world, have a career, have babies later on when I'm older?
- How will having a baby fit in with my social, sporting and community activities?
- Can I afford to raise a child?
- Do I know how much it costs to pay rent, buy food, pay accounts, buy baby things and clothes? Have I done a budget before?
- What support can I realistically expect from family and community? Who will I be able to rely on for support for at least the next few years?
- Will the father really be around to support me? For how long?
- Would I be prepared to bring up a baby by myself if the father left or if my family didn't support me?
- Will my friends hang around?
- Am I ready to give up my personal freedom, for now and the future?

Talk to a doctor or other person you trust, a family planning clinic, youth centre or social worker if you need to discuss your decision making. Whatever the choices you make, you need to be respected, acknowledged and supported. You make the best decisions you can at the time you make them for your situation, resources and wellbeing.

Check out 'Learning More' at the back of the book for more info.

STI reality check (sexually transmissible infections)

Sex is a natural, wonderful part of life. And we all want what comes naturally. Right? Wrong! STIs are a natural thing too. These bugs that cause infections generally have been around for almost as long as humans! They have adapted into sophisticated little critters, and they even share our beds and bodies when we let them. So they cannot be underestimated!

It's important, though, that no matter what kind of sex you are having, you use protection. STIs do not discriminate according to sexual activity. Consent and safety are just as important in all relationships.

Here's the good news about STIs: most of them can be treated or managed, and some can be cured; most STIs can be detected quite simply and painlessly; and most can be prevented. The not-so-good news about STIs: some can be life-threatening if not detected and treated; some cannot be cured; many cause infertility if left undetected and untreated; and some have no or low physical symptoms. All body fluids carry the risk of transmitting an STI or two.

CONDOMS—THE BEST STI BARRIER OF THEM ALL!

You've probably heard it all before, but it's worth saying again . . . condoms can prevent most STIs from being passed on. Condoms provide the *best* and *cheapest* protection on the market so far. And that's for *all* one-on-one sex, whether oral, anal or vaginal.

Condoms and lube are a match made in heaven. And it's fun. Lube is waterbased and with a little imagination is built for great foreplay! You can get non-latex condoms for those who have latex allergies. Check the web and order online (discreet packaging, I am told).

'WHAT IS ONE FUTURE ACHIEVEMENT I HAVE FOR MYSELF? WHAT ARE THE FIRST THREE STEPS TOWARDS ACHIEVING IT?'

STI SYMPTOMS AND TESTS

It's important to stay in tune with your body and give it the attention it needs. If anything worries you, don't hesitate to see a doctor. This list contains very general symptoms that you can look out for:

- burning or pain during peeing
- abnormal smelly discharge from your genitals
- pelvic pain
- bumps, lumps or blisters
- abnormal pain during sex
- rash on hands, feet or stomach.

Getting tested for STIs is a responsible and healthy thing to do. It is not a sign of promiscuity or cheating. When you go to your doctor for an STI check, they will take a vaginal swab and send it to a lab for testing. This will involve a pelvic check. They will collect a sample of mucus from your vagina. If you have a sore, they will need to touch this gently to get a cell sample as well. This might hurt a little so you need to be a bit brave. But remember, your doctor has done this countless times before so you don't have to feel embarrassed. Your doctor should be kind, non-judgemental, explain everything clearly, and not hurry you.

Getting tested and having the all clear does not mean you can have unprotected sex or that you are totally free from any infection. There are STIs that cannot be routinely tested so don't run the risk of spreading something even you don't know about.

Getting tested and being told you have an STI means you've been responsible and got tested. You can now make decisions about what you do next with that information and seek some support. You can take the initiative to minimise exposure to STIs with future sexual partners by using condoms. You may need to inform a person that you have an STI before you have sex with them. You can look after your health. It's an invitation to take care of you!

This list gives you a basic idea about what the various STIs are. You can check out more comprehensive stuff online or ask your doctor.

Chlamydia—This is very common in young people and easily treated and cured with antibiotics. Often there are no symptoms in girls (who are affected worse than guys) but some symptoms in guys. It can cause infertility if left untreated.

Gonorrhoea—This is very common in MSM (men who have sex with men—not necessarily gay guys!). It is easily treated and cured with antibiotics. There are few symptoms, sometimes none if you're unlucky. It can cause infertility if left untreated.

Syphilis—This is easily treated and cured with antibiotics. It can be life-threatening if left untreated. Symptoms can be a rash on your palms, feet and torso, or a sore on your genitals—do not ignore.

Herpes—There are two types—herpes type I (cold sores usually on the lip of your mouth) and herpes type II (generally on your genitals). Both come out like blisters, then turn into sores. Both can be transmitted by skin-to-skin contact. Type I can also be on your genitals (ouch!) and type II can occur on your mouth area (yewh!)—this can happen with oral sex. Really, really common virus. Most people have been exposed to it but may not know. Can be managed (keep the sore outbreaks in check) by staying healthy but cannot be cured. You have the virus forever.

Warts/HPV—This is a family of 'wart' or human papilloma viruses. Not all strains show warts—the sneaky high-risk ones may have no lumpy signs at all. Some strains cause changes in cells in the cervix (entrance to the uterus) and may cause cervical cancer (which is very serious and can be life-threatening if left untreated). Sometimes a woman's immune system can fight the virus, sometimes not. Girls can get a vaccine for certain strains. But even with the vaccine, you MUST still have regular pap smears (the test to show if cells around your cervix have changed—if so it might indicate cancerous cells). The vaccine only covers some strains, not all, that can cause cervical cancer. Getting a vaccine means going to your doctor for a course of three injections over six months. It's certainly easier and better than risking cervical cancer!

Pubic lice (crabs)—These little insects stick to your pubes to party, especially when you're having sex! They itch so you can't miss 'em! Easily treated with special washing lotion.

Have to wash all bed linen, nighties and undies with hot water.

HIV—Human immunodeficiency virus (HIV) is transferred from person to person via blood and other bodily fluids through any breaks in the skin. HIV cannot be cured but, if someone is HIV positive, it can be managed with medication to keep them relatively well, like managing a chronic illness. HIV can lead to AIDS, which is serious and life-threatening. HIV infection may have no obvious symptoms for a long time. You cannot tell if someone has HIV by looking at them. Initially, the first signs of infection might look like a bad flu. However, it can be detected easily through a blood test (usually two to be sure) from 12 weeks after possible exposure to the virus, such as unprotected sexual intercourse. The test is confidential and there is a lot of support for people who are HIV-positive. PEP (post-exposure prophylaxis) are special prescription drugs that can be used to reduce the immediate chance of infection if there has been recent exposure to the virus. It's not a cure once you are infected and it's not 100 per cent effective. It also has significant side-effects. Go to your doctor for more advice.

Hepatitis B—This is a virus which can make your liver seriously ill. Transmitted by infected body fluids. Your body can sometimes clear it through the immune system. Few symptoms but look out for excessive tiredness and yellowish skin. There is no cure but treatments are available. The good news is that a vaccine (series of three needles) is available.

Trichomoniasis—It's a common vaginal infection that causes itching and stinging in the vagina with a smelly discharge. Can cause infertility if left untreated. Easily treated with antibiotics.

'CAN I BE REALLY HONEST WITH MYSELF AND OTHER PEOPLE WITH THE THINGS THAT TRULY MATTER?'

MYTHS ABOUT STIs

MYTH: I can tell if someone else has an STI.
REALITY: You cannot tell if someone has an STI (or HIV).

MYTH: I will always know if I have an STI.
REALITY: You won't always know if you have an STI because some don't have symptoms that alert you to infection.

MYTH. You can't get an STI the first time you have sex
REALITY: You can catch an STI any time you have unprotected sex, and that includes the first time.

MYTH: If you have sex with healthy people, then you can't catch an STI.
REALITY: A lot of healthy people have STIs—some know and some don't.

MYTH: Condoms have holes and don't really prevent STIs or pregnancy anyway.
REALITY: Condoms have been tested and are the safest form of prevention from most STIs. They are also very reliable against pregnancy.

MYTH: If I'm on the pill, then I won't catch an STI.
REALITY: The pill does not prevent STIs.

MYTH: If we just do oral sex, then I won't get an STI and I can't pass one on.
REALITY: You can get and pass on STIs with oral sex.

MYTH: If I get an STI, then I'll be seen to be a slut.
REALITY: STIs do not make you a slut. Being honest about having an STI is very important and shows that you look after yourself and respect your sexual partner.

WHAT IS A URINARY TRACT INFECTION?

A urinary tract infection (UTI) is an infection of the urinary tract, which includes your 'pee equipment'—urethra, ureters, bladder and kidneys. It is a very common infection. It is caused when bacteria (usually e-coli from your anus) enters your urethra and moves up to the bladder and possibly the kidneys.

The symptoms of UTI usually include:

- » a strong urge to urinate but without being able to pass urine
- » a burning or painful sensation when urinating
- » cloudy or dark and unusually smelly urine
- » lower back pain, like you've sprained a muscle
- » chills and possibly fever
- » abdominal and pelvic pain.

Often, girls get a UTI through having sex. This is because in women the urethra is close to the anal opening. The urethra is also relatively small and bacteria from the anus can access the urinary tract fairly easily.

There are some simple things you can do to avoid UTIs. When urinating, wipe yourself from front to back, not the other way. Drink lots of water. Don't wear synthetic undies or clothes that are tight around the crotch. Try to urinate shortly after sex. This flushes out the urethra of any bacteria before they settle in.

It's important to get UTIs treated sooner rather than later as they can get complicated and cause bigger problems, like a kidney infection. An STI can be mistaken for a UTI so you must see your doctor. They will ask for a urine sample to diagnose a UTI. A simple dose of antibiotics can clear it up quickly. Eating healthy food and drinking plenty of water is very healthy for your water works.

TRICKY QUESTIONS

Q Can I use Vaseline, moisturiser and vegetable oil as a lubricant?

A Oils, moisturisers and Vaseline make condoms weak and breakable. Use lube designed for the purpose.

Q Is kitchen plastic wrap as good as a condom if we're caught short?

A Kitchen plastic wrap is totally useless as a barrier to pregnancy and STIs.

Q Won't people think I'm a slut if I carry condoms?

A Carrying condoms is smart thinking. You are considerate and aware. If you have unprotected sex, you may end up with the problem of having an STI or an unplanned pregnancy in the absence of condoms.

Q If my boyfriend pulls out, will I become pregnant?

A Withdrawal has a poor success record in the contraception stakes. If you really don't see yourself pushing a baby stroller in the short term, then reconsider other more reliable contraceptive options.

Q Can tampons block semen and stop me getting pregnant?

A Do not have sex while using a tampon. It's not safe sex and it might hurt. It will not be effective as a contraceptive.

Chapter 7

Being Safe

'Girls don't want to feel vulnerable. But sometimes they do.'

'Little by little he started isolating me. I couldn't talk with my friends, he got angry and upset when I spoke to anyone else . . . things got worse. When I tried to go out, he would then hit me. I was so shocked and scared.'

'My friend said that things were okay for a while but then her boyfriend just got demanding and expected her to be wherever he was. She was scared to hang out with us in case he got angry. He seemed so nice at the start though. Who would have thought something good could go so wrong?'

The truth is that many girls experience unwanted pressure to have sex and some girls give in to doing things they don't want to. Sometimes in life you need to be strong and stand up against the pressure. Knowing what is right and what is wrong for you is important. You can only rely on yourself to make decisions about things like sex, so have trust in yourself, your personal strength to know and act on what is okay and what is not, and the good advice and support you acquire along the way from people who care for you.

There are rules about sex to keep people safe. But despite these, a lot of girls, sadly, experience abuse. If that's you, you need to know what to do to regain your power and feel safe again. Being strong and safe is something that you can do for yourself, and you deserve support and can ask for it whenever you want or need to have it. You have a right to regain control of your situation. Any abuse you experience is not your fault, you did not create it and you can accept support to change the way things are.

Girl power

Ever get that feeling when you're watching a scary or suspenseful movie that something bad is about to happen? You can just *feel* it. It's the same when you find yourself in a place or situation that isn't safe. You'll feel it or hear an inner voice that says something like: 'I'm really not comfortable. It feels unsafe, so I need to get outta here.' If you find yourself in a tricky or scary situation, listen to yourself. If need be say, loud and clear, 'No', 'Go away' or 'I'm leaving'.

This is something you can practise. Do it now. Breathe in and say 'No' loudly. Say it more loudly. And then more loudly again. What does saying no feel like? Practise it in your bedroom, in the shower, while walking to school—whenever you've got some privacy. If necessary, just tell people around you that you're just practising; in any case, having people hear you is very good practice. When you have *that* feeling, the last thing you need to be is quiet—and it will come naturally if you need to say no for real.

LOVE RULES

R Responsible
U Universal
L Laws
E Ensuring
S Safety

Love rules exist to keep people safe and responsible and are generally universal. By birth, you are entitled to:

- freedom to choose
- care, protection and safety
- access to information
- equality and non-discrimination
- quality of life
- social participation
- respect.

YOUR SUPER POWERS

You have secret super powers. Yes, you do! If you concentrate, your body can do a lot of things to access your own personal power. Here's a little test. (You'll need a friend to help with this one.)

Step 1: Stand with one arm at right angles to your body.

Step 2: Ask your friend to force your arm down to your side. Use your arm muscles to resist. Keep trying. Hard?

Step 3: Now try it again, but really concentrate first by imagining a line of steel running from the floor, up through your feet, through to the tip of your raised arm. Keep imagining and breathing into your belly.

Step 4: Ask your friend to push your arm down again while you resist.

Did you both feel a difference? Did you find it easier for you the second time to hold your arm up and resist, and harder for your friend to push your arm down? You are more powerful without having to try harder.

This is the power inside you when you use your concentration and imagination to make yourself strong. If you practise concentrating and imagining yourself strong, then you can be much more powerful in looking after yourself, especially if you are by yourself and in a tricky situation.

You can do a few things to help you be strong and in control while going out:

- Going out does not mean putting out. A date is not a promise for sex.
- Go out with a group, or at least one other friend who you know and trust so you can look out for each other if one gets into a sticky situation.
- Take your mobile, have it charged and with enough credit.
- Take enough money to get home in a taxi just in case.
- Be careful who you invite to your home and be wary of going back to their place. Assaults most often happen in private homes.
- Buy your own drinks. Often drink spiking (adding something to make you feel woozy, or worse) happens when someone else is in control of the drinks. So don't leave your drink; this makes it easy for someone to spike it.
- Trust your inner voice. If it feels weird, scary or just plain icky, it is. Don't stick around.
- Flirt if you want to but know your boundaries. Don't let a bum pat turn into a front pat. Be aware and say STOP if you need to, and leave if you have to.
- Be picky with your guys. If he's not on his absolute best behaviour at first, then it's just downhill from there, honey.
- Don't fall for crappy one-liners. If you're his 'one and only sweet thang, queen dream, lerve machine with sugar on top', he's pulled that line before. He'll move on, and so will you.
- Don't put up with any kind of bribery or manipulation ('I'll buy you a drink if you kiss me' stuff). Focus on your power and what is right and good for you. If someone tries to pressure you, practise your own witty one-liners to get out of the situation.

Most importantly, look after yourself and look after your friends. If you feel uncomfortable and pressured, then go home—your home, that is.

'CAN I TALK TO MY FRIENDS ABOUT DATE SAFETY AND CAN WE COUNT ON EACH OTHER FOR SUPPORT?'

Abusive relationships

Abusive behaviour comes in many ugly shapes and sizes, like:

A Aggression and physical violence
B Blaming, denying, minimising
U Using 'love' to control
S Sexual abuse and insults
I Intimidation
V Verbal attacks
E Economic control

A guy can abuse you and not necessarily touch you. If a guy tries to control you, coerce you, own you, compromise you, intimidate you, put you down in any way or take away your supports and those that care for you, he is abusing you.

An abuser often keeps tabs on you, blames you for their abusive behaviour, makes fun of you, cuts you off from other people and criticises you. Do not try to change him. That won't work. You can, however, change your situation.

If you are in an abusive relationship, you should TALK :

T Tell someone you trust.
A Act quickly and organise support.
L Leave. Nothing is worth sticking around for.
K Know you are strong enough to handle it.

CYCLE OF VIOLENCE

Violence often keeps girls trapped in abusive relationships. People who are prone to abusing their partners will choose people who are easy for them to abuse and keep them trapped in this situation. The violence is consciously constructed to maintain abusive control over the other person. The abuse is directed in a way that may not be obvious but still keeps a girl intimidated and scared. Survivors of abuse are often convinced that their partner cannot control themselves. However, an abuser knows what they are doing and they can control their behaviour. They might try to convince you that they cannot live without you and that they rely on you to help them. The dangers of staying in the relationship are very real for girls who experience abuse. If you fear your partner at any time, or feel you are constantly vigilant about keeping the peace to avoid a reaction, you may be experiencing an abusive relationship. If you think you might be in an abusive relationship, this is what it might look like:

1. TENSION STAGE

YOU FEEL: anxious, worried, like it's going to blow, on 'tenterhooks'

ABUSER: manipulative, acts out abusive control, planning his moves to hurt you

2. EXPLOSION STAGE

YOU FEEL: terrified, fear, stuck, immobilised

ABUSER: yells, screams, is violent, hits or threatens to hurt you or hurt and control you in some way

3. REMORSE STAGE

YOU FEEL: tender, scared, relieved, wary, forgiving

ABUSER: gives gifts, promises not to do it again, begs you to not leave, he's scared of being caught

GO BACK TO 1—IT STARTS ALL OVER AGAIN . . .

If you feel belittled, controlled, self-loathing, inadequate, helpless or desperate in a relationship, it is certainly not for you and you need to TALK (see above). You need to acknowledge the warning signs and act on them in order to end the abuse. If other people suggest you may be in an abusive relationship, listen to them. You need to seek advice and support.

'WHO COULD I TALK TO IF I NOTICED A PATTERN OF ABUSE IN MY LIFE OR A FRIEND'S LIFE?'

Calling it what it is: Date rape

'I was out with a guy and I think I had too much to drink. I can remember him holding me down and having sex with me. I'm not sure what to do now. I'm feeling really messed up.'

Date rape is when someone is forced to have sexual intercourse with a person they know. Rape is about power, not about sex.

If you have experienced date rape, you need to do these things:

» Know it is not your fault. No one invites or asks to be assaulted, abused or raped. Someone you had trusted abused that trust and forced you to do something you did not want. Do not blame yourself.

» Own your feelings—you might be feeling shock, hurt, guilt, ashamed, 'dirty', invaded, angry. Your feelings have every right to be there. And they will change over time.

» Get support. When and how you do that is up to you. Sometimes it's easier to get help sooner rather than later. Talk to someone you trust. That could be a counsellor, police, lawyer, friend or family member. There are phone-line supports if you cannot talk to someone face-to-face right now. You are entitled to support and care at any time.

» See a doctor. They will talk to you about STI and HIV checks. The doctor can provide you with emergency contraception and will talk to you about taking forensic evidence. You may not want to go to court now, but if you change your mind later then the court will need the evidence to support your case.

» Understand your legal rights. You may want to press charges or not. You may want to get an order to prevent that person from being near you. Consider your options. Get advice.

If you are under 16 years of age, it is important for you to tell someone about the assault as it's also illegal for someone to try to have sex with you under this age. Tell a parent, carer or older person you trust. Lifeline and Kids Helpline are free and confidential services—so there's always someone you can talk to.

Online and out there

Online, you are dealing with other, real-life people—their personalities, desires, strengths, weaknesses and warts, both seen or unseen. Online communication needs some smart thinking. When you've met someone online, it can feel like a full-on 'relationship' and true love. Online gives the impression that the relationship is exclusive and there is no one else but the two of you. It can feel exciting and that there is an intensity and chemistry 'shared'. Online can be a real buzz and your body goes through the hormone drive as if you were meeting face-to-face. There may not be physical sex, but it feels like the promise could be there. Best of all, it's 'instant' with the 'real thing' happening in a squillionth of a second. The other person can seem loving, generous, caring and say ALL THE RIGHT THINGS.

Except you haven't actually really met . . .

Going online from your cosy little room can be fun . . . and scary. The icky reality is that even weirdos know how to use the internet. They can seem completely okay, especially online. They can be very sneaky in promoting themselves and looking hot! Smart girls (like you!) need to know what to say and what NOT to say; to trust your gut feelings and know when to tell someone to 'log off'!

The bottom line is that you can't suss the other person out face-to-face. People can misread what is being said and there is no body language to help you work out someone's real intention. You get stuff sent to you that you don't want and didn't ask for. You can give too much away at the touch of a button and you can lose power over what you send. Anything you send can be sent on and used by other people.

Too many people today seem to communicate online instead of face-to-face—not healthy. People *do* tell lies online. How would you know? Some people also hurt people online through scams and tricks by using their personal details to rip them off. Cyber-weirdos can and do abuse young people. They use online anonymity to do scary, illegal things like 'groom' young people (and children) for sexual exploitation.

To be cyber-safe:

» Don't just believe everything you read. You might be honest and trustworthy, but other people may not be.
» Never give away your personal details such as your real name, home address, bank details, home or mobile phone number, or your school or workplace.
» If an onliner asks you to give them your private details, don't.
» Don't meet an onliner face to face. If you do, *never* meet them on your own. Take a friend. Meet in a public place.

- Tell an onliner that someone else knows you are online and they are watching. Check their reaction.
- Don't let another person take pictures of you to put on the net.
- Don't keep it a secret. Tell someone about your contacts.
- If you get porn or insulting messages, do not respond. Contact the service provider.

'HOW CAN I KEEP MYSELF EMOTIONALLY SAFE AND STRONG?'

Break-ups and endings

Even though it can be difficult, there are times when a relationship has to end. The world is full of change—everywhere and all the time. It's not about stopping change (that's impossible). It's about coping with change and being strong, courageous and a girl with integrity and personal skill when change means the ending of a relationship.

If you break up with them:

- Be kind and maintain your integrity.
- Know your reasons and explain them.
- Create space—don't see each other for a while.
- Be open to friendship, but later on down the track.
- Do it face to face, not by text or email.
- Say good things about them.
- Respect what you had and don't gossip about it.

If they break up with you:

- Whether you are ready or not, it is time to move on. Crying and saying it's not fair may feel true and real for you. It may not be fair right now but over time it will be clear to you why it didn't work out.
- Don't lose your cool, stay calm and breathe.
- Listen to them, even if you don't agree.
- Agree to be open to friendship, but later on if it feels right.
- Agree to keep some space between you and them.
- Tell them what you feel.
- Cry but don't cling to them.
- Call a friend for support.

Crying is a release and a great healing process. Handling a breakup requires a few good healthy coping strategies, like:

Do (the good stuff):

» Allow yourself to own your feelings.
» Relax and find a safe place in yourself.
» Be with your friends.
» Seek support and talk to someone.
» Keep up an exercise routine and eat well.
» Treat yourself kindly and do nice things for yourself.
» Learn from it and move on eventually.

Do not do (the bad stuff):

» Drink alcohol or take drugs to obliterate the pain.
» Treat yourself like a sinking ship—you will recover and you need time to mend.
» Do not let your negative emotions play mutiny over your life—the relationship was not okay but you are.
» Dive into a 'rebound' relationship.
» Blame yourself.

TRICKY QUESTIONS

Q **What if I'm getting hassled online?**

A Don't respond or engage with the person in any way. It's not easy, but they feed off your responses—so 'starve' them. Keep all the emails. Put them in a separate folder—they can be used as evidence against the person. They can get into lots of trouble if they persist. Email the service provider and let them know the email address of the bully. If they get enough complaints, they will close the account down. Get support and tell an adult you trust. It's important to get help. There are also websites that can help you deal with online bullies. Sometimes the internet can be just *too* easy. And that makes people behave in a callous, superficial or thoughtless way which can be quite hurtful. Sometimes people play mind-games online. It's important to have a life offline.

Q **If I change my mind and don't want to have sex, then I'm just a tease.**

A You need to be true to yourself. You can always change your mind—anytime. Do not put up with being put-down. Being called a tease is a put-down and you have the choice to change your mind anytime. You have every reason to say no, as you have every reason to say yes. All your reasons are valid but you are not required to provide a reason for your decision.

Q **I've sent a naked photo of myself to my boyfriend's mobile phone. Someone told me that this was not legal, is that true?**

A Mobile phones have become an important way for young people to communicate. However, sending sexually explicit or naked photos of yourself or other people is illegal and has serious consequences. Many young people misunderstand the laws related to 'sexting' and think that it's fun and flirtatious. Under the current laws in Australia, a young person can be charged if they take a naked photo of themselves and send it to someone else. Photos taken by mobile phone, whether they are sent or unsent into cyberspace, have been used as evidence in court where young people have been charged under laws related to child pornography. Some young people have been listed as sex offenders because of their involvement in either naked or sexual photos taken or sent by mobile phone.

Never underestimate the negative fallout of someone else having a naked or sexual photo of you. They can send it to other people or upload the image onto the internet, which means your family, school, friends, strangers and future employer might also have access to this image of you. Once it's in cyberspace it's out of your control forever. Acknowledge it was an error of judgement to send the image to your boyfriend and ask him to delete it from the phone and his computer. Seek support if you need to and get advice if this situation has gotten out of hand. You deserve to be supported.

Chapter 8

Looking After Your Future

'What should a girl expect? Respect!'

What do you want to have in your life in one month, one year, five years' time? What about in ten years' time? It's hard to imagine, and sometimes thinking even a week ahead can feel complicated. You are making decisions now so that you have a future that you can feel proud of and empowered by when you are 'in your future' later on. Those decisions relate to your education, work, family relationships, partner and sexual relationships, friendships and possibly your work and family life into the future. Most of us construct an idea of what we would like our future to be from our family, friends and special people in our life. Sometimes what we want has absolutely nothing to do with anybody else's work or life experience as you see it now. When someone asks, 'What do you want to be when you grow up?', before you can truthfully answer you must do a lot of research, with support and through lots of trial and error. But there are some things you can make decisions about now that will have a significant impact on your future. If you want some perspective on 'the future', you might want to ask your parents or another trusted adult, 'What did you want from your life when you were my age?' You might be surprised with the response you get. Trust that working out where you are now and what you do is a very useful starting point for where you want to be later on. I suggest you write three things you want to achieve at certain points; say, at one, two and five years. This would be a good start. Keep your achievement list somewhere special and look at it every so often. Are you doing what you need to in order to get where you want to go? Remember to keep your options open.

Looking after your health

This is the boring but important section where we talk about stuff you *need* to know about 'down there'. Here's the deal—if you know, then you can choose. Don't know, can't choose. Which would you prefer? A doctor can talk to you more about this stuff, but it's worth your while to know a few basic details first.

PAP TEST

A pap test is done to check if there are any abnormal or pre-cancerous cells on the entrance of your cervix. Remember the cervix is at the top of your vagina and at the entrance to your uterus (womb). The distance to your cervix from the entrance of your vagina is generally about the length of your middle finger. If you inserted your finger into your vagina and felt your cervix, you would feel that it was similar to the tip of your nose.

Why do you need to get one? Your risk of developing cervical cancer can be reduced by having regular pap tests. If abnormal cells are found early, then they can be watched and treated if necessary. All women aged 18 to 70 need to have a routine pap test every two years.

What causes abnormal cells? Infections, such as the wart virus (HPV), are the main culprit. The wart virus is an STI and is very common among sexually active people. In Australia, the HPV vaccine is free to women less than 26 years of age.

How does a pap test work? Your clinician will need to access your cervix. The way that's done is by you lying on the examination table with your knees up. It's an uncomfortable position for a girl to be in but, remember, your clinician has seen hundreds and maybe thousands of vaginas so they are an expert. They should also be clear and kind and should make you feel safe, comfortable and unhurried.

The clinician will slowly and carefully insert a specially designed plastic or metal 'duck-bill' contraption (a speculum, and it looks just like a duck's bill), which gently creates a space to see the top of your vagina. Remember, your vagina is very muscular and flexible but has few nerve endings. So you just need to just breathe slowly and steadily. It may feel a little unusual (and perhaps a little drafty!) but it should not hurt you if you relax your pelvic muscles. Your clinician will then get a tiny brush with a thin long handle and collect a few of your cervical cells; these will be put on a slide for testing in a lab. It should not hurt.

Your clinician might also have a look to see if everything looks normal as well. After all, you may as well get the whole treatment while you're there! Your clinician will then close and remove the speculum and, voila, your pap test is done!

They might also do a pelvic check by inserting a couple of gloved fingers into your vagina with one hand and pressing gently between your pelvic bones and lower abdomen with the other to see if anything hurts or feels lumpy. It's okay, they know what they're doing. If you feel any pain or discomfort, you need to tell the clinician. Finally, your clinician will ask you to get off the table, get your pants on and tell you how you will get your pap test results, or to how to get any follow up tests they think you might need.

'WHAT IS ONE POSITIVE THING ABOUT MY BODY? HOW WILL I LOOK AFTER IT INTO THE FUTURE?'

DID YOU KNOW?

The word 'pelvis' is Latin for 'basin' because your pelvic area is shaped just like one.

BREAST SENSE—GET IN TOUCH WITH YOUR BOOBS

Now you have probably heard that Kylie Minogue and other famous people have had breast cancer and recovered after treatment to lead successful lives. That's because they found out early! There are many other women who find out too late and become very sick and sometimes die. It's vital that you know how to check your own breasts. After all, no one knows your breasts better than you do.

Your boobs (breasts) are changing all the time but if you feel them regularly, then you will know what is normal and what isn't normal. So this is what you do:

- Stand in front of the mirror with your top and bra off. It's normal to have one breast slightly larger than the other if that is what you see. Check if there are any visible lumps. Check if the skin is puckered like orange skin (not good), or if there is any discharge from the nipple (not good either).
- Your breast area goes to the side under your armpit, down and under your boob, across to your breastbone (in the middle of your chest) and up towards your clavicle (your 'coathanger' bone at the front). Have a feel.
- Start by putting your right arm on the top of your head. Then hold your left hand flat on your right breast and use the flat part of your fingers between the finger pads and palm to check your breast. Press around the breast firmly—that way you will pick up anything unusual. Check out your breast from the nipple (don't worry, it's only you touching it), right into the underarm area. It's really important to check out each area to get a good idea how it feels and what is normal to you (and not normal).
- Then swap sides and check your left breast, putting your left arm on top of your head and feeling with your right hand. Easy!

When do you do it? Hormones can make your breasts lumpier than usual before and during your period. So check them once a month just after your period. If you do it in the shower, then it's private. Soap might make it easier because your hand can glide over your skin.

What if you find a lump? Finding a lump does not mean you panic. The chance of it not being cancer is nine out of 10. And if it is cancer, then you may have caught it early enough for successful treatment. But you *must* see your doctor as soon as you find any unusual lumps. That's why it's important to check yourself regularly.

Looking after your fertility

You may not think you want children now or later on, but you might want to be sure that you did your best to keep yourself healthy enough to possibly have them if you did change your mind in the future. You may not want to go to university now, but you might want to get enough marks at school to allow you to attend if you did suddenly realise there was course at university that inspired you down the track. It's about keep your options open and making room for choices in your life. Choosing to have children later in your life may be one of the best things you do. Keep in mind that your fertility (chances of being able to naturally conceive a baby) decreases significantly as you get into your mid to late 30s. Some women do have babies into their 40s, but the health risks for these women and their babies are much greater. So keep your options open. If babies are on your future plan, then think about having them not too soon and not too late, but at a time when it might be just right for you. STIs left untreated can lead to infertility (not being able to conceive naturally) or make babies sick when they are born.

The reality is that sometimes the most careful girls in the world can still catch an STI. The reason is that some (like herpes and the 'genital wart' virus) can be easily passed on through skin contact while having sex. Other STIs can be passed on through sharing bodily fluids like blood, semen and vaginal fluid. Sexual activity like oral sex can also pass on STIs like herpes.

If you have a smelly discharge, sores, lumps, any pelvic pain, itching, twinges or tingling pain in your genitals, then get it checked out ASAP (as soon as humanly possible). Some STIs are tricky because they have no obvious symptoms and you wouldn't know they were doing damage to your body. That's why it's worth getting checked out for STIs when you go to the doctor or clinic for your routine pap test, or if you feel that something is not quite right in your body. Most STIs can be detected very easily.

The good news is that you can either treat or manage an infection if you get one. Most STIs can be easily treated and cured with antibiotics. A few STIs unfortunately cannot be cured, but have treatments to manage them and keep them from getting worse. Some STIs can be cleared by your healthy immune system without you knowing—but you won't know which ones unless you see your clinician.

The main message is to get yourself checked out and treated early. Don't wait and worry.

'DO I TREAT MY BODY WITH THE SAME RESPECT AS ANY OTHER FAVOURITE POSSESSION?'

The end? The beginning!

You are on an amazing journey—and you definitely need more than just your fave jeans, iPod and mobile phone. You need a steady heart, knowledge of yourself, and your destination clearly in mind. Now you can explore the options, and there are plenty of them out there. This book is one way of working out the horizon from the shimmery haze that might just be a mirage. You start by making that step, then another. Your heart will get strong and you will become sure as you move forward. You're getting ready for a fantastic adventure—your life. Just one thing before you go, don't forget:

Do what you love. Don't compromise. Your heart knows.

Keep yourself safe. Your body is your vehicle for the future. Look after it.

Find some quiet time. Chill out. Relax.

Have fun with your friends. They will remind you of you.

Listen to the other side. Patience is cool.

Trust yourself. Your body knows a lot. Listen to it.

Remember that everything changes. Life is up and down. It will even out eventually.

And send me a postcard!

GO GIRL!

Learning More

BOOKS

These books have helped me at different times in my life and given me insights and support:

The Artist's Way by Julie Cameron.
Barnes and Noble Publishers, 2002.
This is another journey book. It's honest, compassionate and gives you some great ways to reflect on yourself and the world you live in.

Creating Love by John Bradshaw.
Bantam Publishers, 1994.
He is a practical thinker on love and relationships. It has some great little activities in it too.

Facing Love Addiction by Pia Melody.
Harper Collins Publishers, 2002.
This book is about being honest with yourself and how, when we love someone, we can sometimes give ourselves away and hurt at the same time.

Girlosophy: The love survival kit by Anthea Paul.
Allen & Unwin Publishers, 2000.
A book you should have, for fun and feeling good.

Intimacy and Solitude by Stephanie Dowrick.
Womens Press Publishers, 1993.
This lady truly knows her stuff. This book is a wonderful journey book. Once you start it, you need to finish it and you will not be the same afterwards. It's a tool for life.

Journey of the Heart: The path of conscious love by John Welwood.
Harper Collins Publishers, 1996.
A really compassionate author who helps you to be consciously with the person you are with (which is actually yourself).

Looking for Mr Right by Bradley Trevor Grieve.
Andrew McMeel Publishing, 2nd edition 2001.
A funny and clever five-minute book on actually being yourself when it comes to guys!

The Puberty Book by Wendy Darvill and Kelsey Powell. Hachette Australia Publishers, 2007.
This is a fabulously user-friendly book that gives plenty of good honest advice on growing up.

Puberty Girl by Shushann Movsessian.
Allen & Unwin Publishers, 2004.
This is the best book on puberty!

Relationships that Rock by Sue Ostler.
Allen & Unwin Publishers, 2004.
This is a great read if you are looking into choosing your next relationship.

The Sex Doctor by Tracey Cox.
Bantam Publishers, 2005.
Lots of info on sex stuff. Tracey gets into the real nitty gritty; for the mature reader.

WEBSITES

Family planning and reproductive health

For each state and territory of Australia, we are proud to present organisations that have fabulous, unbiased information on contraception, sexual health, pregnancy, sexual health advice and STIs. Check it out.

www.fpnsw.org.au
www.fpq.com.au
www.shinesa.org.au
www.fpwa.org.au
www.shfpact.org.au
www.fpv.org.au
www.familyplanningadvice.com.au
www.mariestopes.com.au
www.au.reachout.com

Sexual relationships

Lots of great support about teen relationships generally and sexual health specifically.

www.yoursexhealth.org
www.likeitis.org.au
www.scarleteen.com
www.glcsnsw.org.au

STIs

Get info now on STIs and how to stay safe sexually.

www.sextxt.org.au
www.istaysafe.com
www.fpnsw.org.au
www.healthinsite.gov.au

HIV/AIDS

Websites on same sex attraction, HIV transmission, how to access info on infection, treatment and risk.

www.acon.org.au
www.fpnsw.org.au
www.multiculturalhivhepc.net.au (in lots of languages)
www.napwa.org.au (support for positive people)

Mental health

Information and great advice on how to look after yourself and your friends. Mental health, anxiety, depression and youth suicide can be prevented. Check out how.

www.au.reachout.com
www.kidshelp.com.au
www.beyondblue.org.au
www.headspace.org.au
www.mmha.org.au (for multilingual information)
www.startts.org.au (for refugees)

Violence, rape and abusive relationships

Everyone deserves comprehensive free and uncomplicated advice when it comes to violence, abuse and sexual assault. Just check out a few websites for information and places to go for more support.

www.dvirc.org.au/whenlove/
www.nswrapecrisis.com.au
www.aboutdaterape.nsw.gov.au/
PH: 1800 RESPECT (1800 737 732) (confidential counselling and information services)

Internet abuse

Don't let an online problem be a silent problem. Seek support. Websites here are a good start.

www.bullyonline.org
www.kidshelp.com.au

Bullying

Do not allow bullying and peer oppression to get you down. There is advice and a lot of support. Speak up and let people know. In the meantime, check out a few sites for extra support. You are not on your own. Believe it.

www.bullyingnoway.com.au
www.bullying.com.au
www.ncab.org.au/bullying/
www.cyh.com (go to 'Teen health', then browse by category 'Society and you')
www.youth.nsw.gov.au/youth_links/links/getting_help/bullying_and_problems_at_school

www.police.nsw.gov.au/community_issues/domestic_and_family_violence/bullying_at_school_and_in_the_home
www.au.reachout.com

Pregnancy choices and the law

Where can you go for non-judgemental and unbiased advice and you know that you are respected? Check out this selection of sites for information and see a doctor and someone you trust to get support.

www.fpnsw.org.au
www.childrenbychoice.org.au
www.mariestopes.com.au
www.sextxt.org.au

Alcohol and other drugs

Get some good advice on drugs and alcohol. Good strong support and sound advice are always there for you when need it. This information is to give you the facts. You decide.

www.yds.org.au
www.adin.com.au (also for treatment and information)
www.headspace.org.au

Life stuff

Want the lowdown on living well and independently? Check this site out for the good stuff.

www.youthcentral.vic.gov.au
www.betterhealth.vic.gov.au

Body health

Start here for good health advice on breast health and how you might be able to actually prevent cancer. Tops tips! This also includes some of the basics of body health.

www.bsnsw.org.au (for breast checks)
www.cancercouncil.com.au (go to 'Preventing cancer' at the top)
www.cancerscreening.gov.au (for cervical screening)
www.betterhealth.vic.gov.au

Gay, lesbian, bisexual, transgender

Check out these sites for advice on health, housing, support, counselling and guidance. Remember, it's about how you love, not who you love.

www.twenty10.org.au
www.avp.acon.org.au
www.gendercentre.org.au
www.glcsnsw.org.au

Aboriginal health

Check out this site for health advice!

www.ahmrc.org.au
www.healthinfonet.ecu.edu.au

Multicultural health

www.mhcs.health.nsw.gov.au (under 'Publications and resources')
www.mmha.org.au (Mental health)

Legal stuff

Get the lowdown on the law and you. These sites are Australian, so check them out.

www.lawstuff.org.au
www.theshopfront.org
www.youthlaw.asn.au

First published in 2011

Allen & Unwin
Sydney, Melbourne, Auckland, London
83 Alexander Street
Crows Nest NSW 2065
Australia
Phone: (61 2) 8425 0100
Fax: (61 2) 9906 2218
Email: info@allenandunwin.com
Web: www.allenandunwin.com

Cataloguing-in-Publication details are available from the National Library of Australia
www.trove.nla.gov.au

ISBN 978 1 74175 143 7

Design by Liz Seymour
Internal photography by iStockphoto and Corbis Images
Illustrations by Davey Mac www.teazer.com.au
Printed in China by 1010 Printing International Limited

10 9 8 7 6 5 4 3 2 1

Sexpectations Boy will help you make healthy, positive choices based on the right information.

Sexpectations talks to guys (and girls) about when to have sex, how sex happens, why you might (or might not) have sex, what does sex feel like and other important things to know if and when a guy has, or is about to have, sex.

But sex isn't just about one person. ***Sexpectations*** goes way past how to put on a condom — it explores the tricky areas of pleasure, desire, relationships and identity, with real life information shared in a straightforward way.

With comments from other guys facing the same experience, ***Sexpectations*** talks honestly and respectfully about the hard questions.

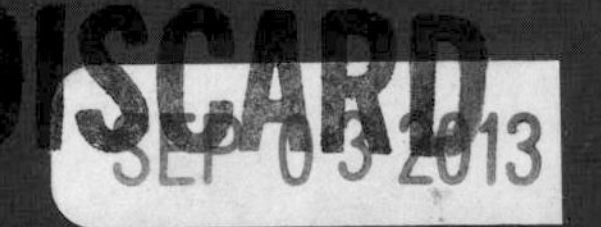

SEXPECTATIONS BOY

CRAIG MURRAY

CONTENTS

About Me

Among other things, I'm a community health worker at an organisation called SHine SA (Sexual Health information networking and education, South Australia). I've been talking about sex for a long time, but in the last 12 years I've been lucky enough to be paid for it!

I started out as a peer educator at SHine SA—this means they trained me to share information with my mates, mostly guys who would never go into a health clinic. Then, as a youth consultant, I was involved in training doctors, nurses and youth workers. I've studied community care (looking after old folks or people with disabilities in their home), youth work, community development and primary healthcare. Plus I've done squillions of courses and workshops related specifically to sexual health.

But I've learned the biggest lessons in life from all the people I've been lucky enough to work with in the community. And from being a dad to two growing and healthy young men.

I'd like to thank Di and Liz at CKSD for their vision and fine taste in writers and my co-writer, Leissa, for her perspective and sense of humour.

The hugest of thanks to all of the guys I've interviewed for this book—Anthony, Chris, Edd, Fernando, Nick, Lud, Jules and Ryan—for sharing their experiences and expectations.

Also heaps of love and thanks to all the folks who have helped me realise what it means to be a man: Amanda, Amy, Anwar, Big A, Bob, Brook, Ember, Jarod, Jim, Jo, John, Jules, Kim, Leigh, Lexton, Lisa, Lynn, Norman, Robbie, Rox, Sonja, Steph, Steve, Steve, Tam, Tiff, Vanessa, as well as all the SHine Folks, SFC and the 'Willdinga' Krew.

Heaps of love to my sons, Chris and Gray, who've taught me so much about life. And extra special thanks and love to my folks May and Tom, for literally making me . . . and teaching me about love.

I'd like to dedicate *Sexpectations Boy* to my late Uncle Fergie—a man among men who taught me the true value of humour; and my gran, 'Old Iron Feest', who taught me that it doesn't matter who you love—'love is love'.

Why use 'partner'?

There are many different names for people we have sex with, it can depend on the type of relationship we have with them—it could be a boyfriend, girlfriend, lover or sex friend . . . or your relationship might not have a name.

I use the word 'partner' because lots of guys have lots of sex with people who aren't their girlfriend, and lots of sex happens outside of a 'traditional relationship'.

To me, 'partner' suggests that sex is something you work together on. It makes me think of equality and respect—a partnership . . . apart from that, using 'partner' instead of 'girlfriend/boyfriend/lover/sex friend/other' saves a lot of words!

Introduction

Sex! What a cool topic . . . but why call a book *Sexpectations*?

Well, sometimes we can be *expected* to know everything there is to know about sex, but rarely get a chance to talk about it in an open, healthy way, or to ask questions like, 'What do I do?', 'What's normal?' And that's just a few of those tricky questions we all have . . .

Sex is one of those things that people are always interested in. If you thought that sex info started and ended with how to put a condom on, think again. In *Sexpectations* we talk about heaps of stuff to do with pleasure, identity, technique, orgasms, myths and realities, and a whole lot more. We also look at what makes sex healthy and what can make it unhealthy—and what to do if anything goes wrong.

And if you have, or hope to have, a girlfriend, we encourage you to flip this book over and have a read of *Sexpectations Girl*. Guys need to know about girls and their bodies, and girls need to know about guys and their bodies, so that we can support each other—after all, we're in this together.

How you think about sex can make a big difference to the sex you have. If you think sex is something that's dirty and shameful, it might be harder to enjoy what you're doing and may prevent you from learning about your body—like what turns you on—and knowing how to keep you (and your partner) safe and happy. If you think sex is a natural, healthy thing, there's a good chance you'll enjoy the sex you have, enjoy healthier relationships, and feel better about yourself too—sounds pretty good to me!

Sexpectations isn't about telling you how to feel or what to do. It is an opportunity to explore some of the highs and lows and the confusing 'in-betweens' of sex. There'll be some answers to questions you may already have—and maybe some answers to questions you hadn't even thought of yet. But most importantly, how you do your thing is up to you, because when it comes to your sex and sexuality, it's all about YOU!

So find a nice spot, get comfy and let's go exploring . . .

Chapter 1

What is Sex?

Sex is . . .

'Doing it.'

'Sexual intercourse.'

'Fun.'

'A way of showing love and intimacy.'

'Okay, but making love is awesome.'

'Something that's all yours—and your partner's.'

'Scary.'

'The name of the game.'

'Sexeriffic!'

'All some people think about.'

'Isn't that important to me.'

'Sexy.'

THERE'S A WHOLE HEAP OF STUFF TO EXPLORE ABOUT SEX, but for now let's start with that very basic question—what is sex?

For some guys, it's a huge part of their life, for others it doesn't matter much at all. Some see sex as way more than the physical act of kissing, sliding and sucking—it can be a way of sharing your mind, body and soul with your partner; it can be a great stress reliever; it can be a spiritual experience. It is a way of making babies, and it can be a way of celebrating your love or even life in general. The common perception of sex is having penetrative, penis-in-vagina sex, and by doing that you are losing your virginity. But what about oral sex or anal sex? Are they still sex?

So much goes into creating our attitude towards sex—our experiences, our learning, our identity. Then there's all these other factors like our:

» emotions—our experience of love, belonging, connectedness, self-esteem
» body—physical stuff like lust, abilities, body image
» mind—education and knowledge
» spirit—thoughts on transcending the material world, religion, rituals or rules
» culture—what we think about gender roles, attitudes towards sex, and the laws.

'WHAT DO I THINK SEX IS, AND WHAT INFLUENCES WHAT I BELIEVE?'

Why do people have sex?

The usual response to this question is: 'Because they can—it feels good'! But the main reason people give for having sex is that they are attracted to the other person. There are many reasons for having sex, and not all are associated with feeling good. Some can lead to a whole heap of disappointment, even danger. I've also heard of some pretty scary motives—people using sex to hurt or get back at someone.

Your reason for having sex can affect not only your relationships but also your sexual, mental, physical and spiritual health—in fact, your enjoyment of life.

ASK YOURSELF 'WHY DO I WANT TO HAVE SEX?'

This is also a good question to ask your partner because confusion over expectations can lead to disappointing sex and the relationship breaking down.

HEALTH BENEFITS OF SEX

Sex can relieve stress, boost immunity, burn calories, improve self-esteem, improve cardio-vascular health, reduce pain, increase intimacy, strengthen pelvic floor muscles, help you sleep and reduce the risk of prostate cancer in men . . . and it feels good too !

SEXPECTATION

Asking yourself why you want to have sex might seem like a weird question, and the answer might change from day to day for you, but it can be a good reality check to make sure you're setting yourself realistic expectations.

What are the rules of the game?

When it comes to sex, there are laws and rules—legal and social—that are meant to keep everyone safe. It's really important that you know what these are, especially as they vary depending on where you live and your background.

LAWS ABOUT SEX

Laws about sex are set out by the government and reflect community attitudes. You have no choice about these; they are put in place to protect everyone. You can check them out at the National Children's and Youth Law Centre website, www.lawstuff.org.au, to see what the laws are for your area. But here's some essential information you need to know:

» *Consent*—This is a BIG issue and I suggest you make it one of your personal rules to get super clear about consent. Consent means someone agrees to have sex. It's really important and if someone says no then that means no. If someone has been tricked or threatened or blackmailed or manipulated into having sex—this is not consent—this is coercion. If someone is drunk or out of it on drugs they can't consent to sex—if they're too drunk to say no, then they're too drunk to say yes. Sometimes it can be hard to ask for consent. Sometimes it can be hard to say no.

  You don't have to have a signed permission slip, but you can ask 'Is this okay?', 'Are you sure you want to do this?' And look out for body language, even if they're saying yes, what is their body saying?

  It can be frustrating if you're really keen to have sex and your partner's not, but dealing with a bit of frustration is a lot better than having sex with someone who doesn't want to have sex with you. You might get some respect for not pushing the point and get a reputation as a respectful pleasure seeker . . . and masturbation can be a great way to relieve some of that frustration.

» *Age of consent*—This is the age you must be before you can legally have sexual intercourse. It's illegal to have sex with someone younger than this age. (See information in girls' section on p. 13.)

  These are the same for heterosexual and homosexual sex. Queensland has set the age of consent for anal sex to 18.

» *Sex with family members*—You can only have sex with someone if they are not part of your family, and your family includes your parents, brothers, sisters, uncles, aunties, grandparents, and may also include your cousins and step-relatives.

» *Sex with teachers or people in power*—Across Australia you must be over 18 to have sex with someone in a position of trust or power, eg teacher, socialworker, youthworker, etc. There are often rules set by the institutions these people work for.

» *Sex with animals*—It's illegal to have sex with animals, and this may also bring up charges of animal cruelty.

» *Sex in public*—Sex in public is illegal, and you'll need to understand the definition of public and private spaces in the laws of your region.

SOCIAL RULES ABOUT SEX

Social rules are defined by your family, friends, culture, community or religion. They are different for everyone. They might relate to whether you can have sex before marriage, who you can have sex with, where you can have sex and what kind of sex you can have. They are guided by ethics—the *sense* of what's right and what's wrong. Some of these rules will make sense for you but, because sexuality is such an individual thing, some won't.

When you include someone else in your sexual activity, you also include their rules about sex. This may take some negotiation. Never assume your rules are their rules—talk about it, be clear about what stuff is okay, what's a maybe and what is definitely a no go.

When you start ignoring your own sense of what's right and what's wrong, you can start to resent the other person. When you ignore the other person's rules, you have to ask yourself how much you really care about them. Either way, safety goes out the window and safety is essential to healthy sex and relationships.

Relationships rules

What are your rules when it comes to:

- safer sex?
- sex with an ex-partner?
- sex with a friend's ex-partner?
- flirting?
- conflict? What does fighting fair mean to you?
  No violence of any kind is a really good start.
- open honest communication?
- being clear about what you're fighting about?
- being open to the idea that sometimes we might be wrong?
- dealing with stuff as it comes up?

How do we learn about sex?

You've been learning about sex from the moment you were born. It's thought that as soon as a baby realises they can control those things stuck on the end of their arms (hands), they start touching their genitals. Why? Because it feels good! Unfortunately, some learning experiences aren't that good; some might be bad and some confusing—especially if there's no one to help you make sense of it all. What you learn about sex can influence your expectations as well as the sex you have.

SEX EDUCATION IS EVERYWHERE . . .

You learn a lot about how to be in the world from the people in your life—your cultural background, friends and family—and by watching the way men and women treat each other. The people around you have been giving you unconscious lessons in how to be a man—the scary and exciting thing is you're influencing others too!

'What kind of messages am I giving other people about me?'

How you talk and think about sex can affect how safe people around you feel. Be supportive of those who open up to you with their feelings about sex. If you pay them out, it can send the message that it's not okay to talk about sex. If you share some of your own uncertainties or fears, it can make for a much stronger friendship.

SEX EDUCATION IN SCHOOL

When I was in Year 7 a teacher told us there was a TV show on that night which would be good to watch. It was called 'No one wants an unwanted baby'. The title, apart from being really obvious, sent out a pretty strong negative message about sex. I ended up watching it in the dark, terrified that either my parents or my older brothers would catch me—not the most positive introduction to sex ed. Thankfully, sexual education in schools has come a long way—but there's still a long way to go.

School sex education is often left out or covered in an embarrassed rush. Frequently, teachers aren't supported to explore the confusing areas of sexuality like sexual identity, power, pleasure, values and attitudes, so they stick to the fact-based stuff like sexually transmissible infections (STIs) and contraception. This can give a biased view of sex when sex ed only deals with the negative consequences of sex.

'WHAT IS YOUR SCHOOL SEX EDUCATION LIKE?'

Try to think about what is talked about, what is left out and what messages are being given. Is sex an okay thing?

SEX IN THE MEDIA

The media—internet, TV, radio, books, magazines, phones, etc.—have all been trying their best to pass on their version of sexuality. There's no escaping it. Movies, soap operas, dating services, adult phone lines, websites (with mobile phones they can reach you wherever you go), advertising—all of them run by the old saying, 'Sex sells': 'Watch/buy our product and you'll be more attractive and therefore get more sex.'

The media loves the extremes of sex—from the good old fairytale romance to the shock horror stories. The media doesn't like reality—there's rarely any negotiation of condom use, farting in bed, juggling relationships with school or work, talk of masturbation or keeping a hard-on. And then there's porn . . .

When it comes to finding out about the mechanics of sex, what goes where, etc., pornography is where a lot of guys get their information. I'm not saying that it's bad or good . . . I encourage you to decide for yourself what's healthy and respectful and what to avoid. And this advice applies to all media, even this book. If you want to question the information in this book, that's great—it means you're involved in your own sexual education! We'll be talking more about pornography later.

What do we think sex is?

In Australia, levels of sexual abuse, sexual assault, relationship violence, STIs and unwanted pregnancies are way too high. In countries like Holland and Denmark, levels of sexual violence, unplanned pregnancy and STIs are a lot lower than in countries like Australia, England and the United States. Some people believe this is due to their comprehensive sex and relationship education.

So we believe the more you learn about what sex is, and the more open and honest the people you talk to about sex are, the better equipped you will be to understand the myths and realities about sex, to work out what sex means to you and to be a sexually healthy person. For us, *sex is* a pleasurable, natural, healthy and good thing.

'WHAT IS SEX TO ME?'

Sex positive—a great way to be

Being 'sex positive' means being okay with whatever people get up to. So long as they're okay with what they're doing, and it's not illegal or exploiting anyone, it's totally fine. It doesn't need explaining or justifying to anyone. Even if you're not interested in sex at all, as long as you support other people in doing what they want to do, you can still be sex positive.

The good thing about this attitude is that when you make it safer for other people to do what they want, you make it safer for yourself too!

'SO HOW MUCH DO I KNOW ABOUT MY MIND AND BODY?'

TRICKY QUESTIONS

Q Is the age of consent the same for homosexual and heterosexual sex?

A The age of consent varies across Australia but the laws apply equally to heterosexual and homosexual sex.

Q I want to masturbate, but I live in a big family—how can I get privacy?

A Privacy can be especially hard to get when you share a room. It might be possible to work out a time-share arrangement—so everyone has a time when they have the room to themselves. Is it possible to have a lock on your bedroom door to give you a little peace of mind? You can forget about interruptions and enjoy your wank. You can also get some privacy in your bathroom and toilet. Privacy is good for your mental health too, so getting a bit of space for yourself is a really healthy thing to do.

Q What if you've only had negative experiences of sex and relationships?

A It's really important to get information and support—find out what healthy sex and relationships look and feel like. Can you think of any positive relationships around you—what makes them work? Watch how the people treat each other. It's kind of like practising respect

It can be really hard if all the relationships around you are pretty negative too—it might seem like a positive healthy relationship is an impossibility. But the reality is that lots of people learn and grow from their negative experiences and get really clear about the kind of relationship they don't want.

What made your past experiences bad or negative? That's important to know if you want to find out how to avoid them in the future. What could you do differently in your next relationship? I guess that's what life's all about—learning from your experiences.

Chapter 2

Body Bits

'Sometimes when I was getting turned on, it would feel like I'd leave my body—it was like I was floating, watching someone else that looked like me.'

'I hate it when my partner just focuses on my dick—we've talked about it but they keep on coming back to it. I mean I do like it but I love my thighs being stroked too—and my feet give me an electric chill when they are rubbed right.'

'How big is big enough?'

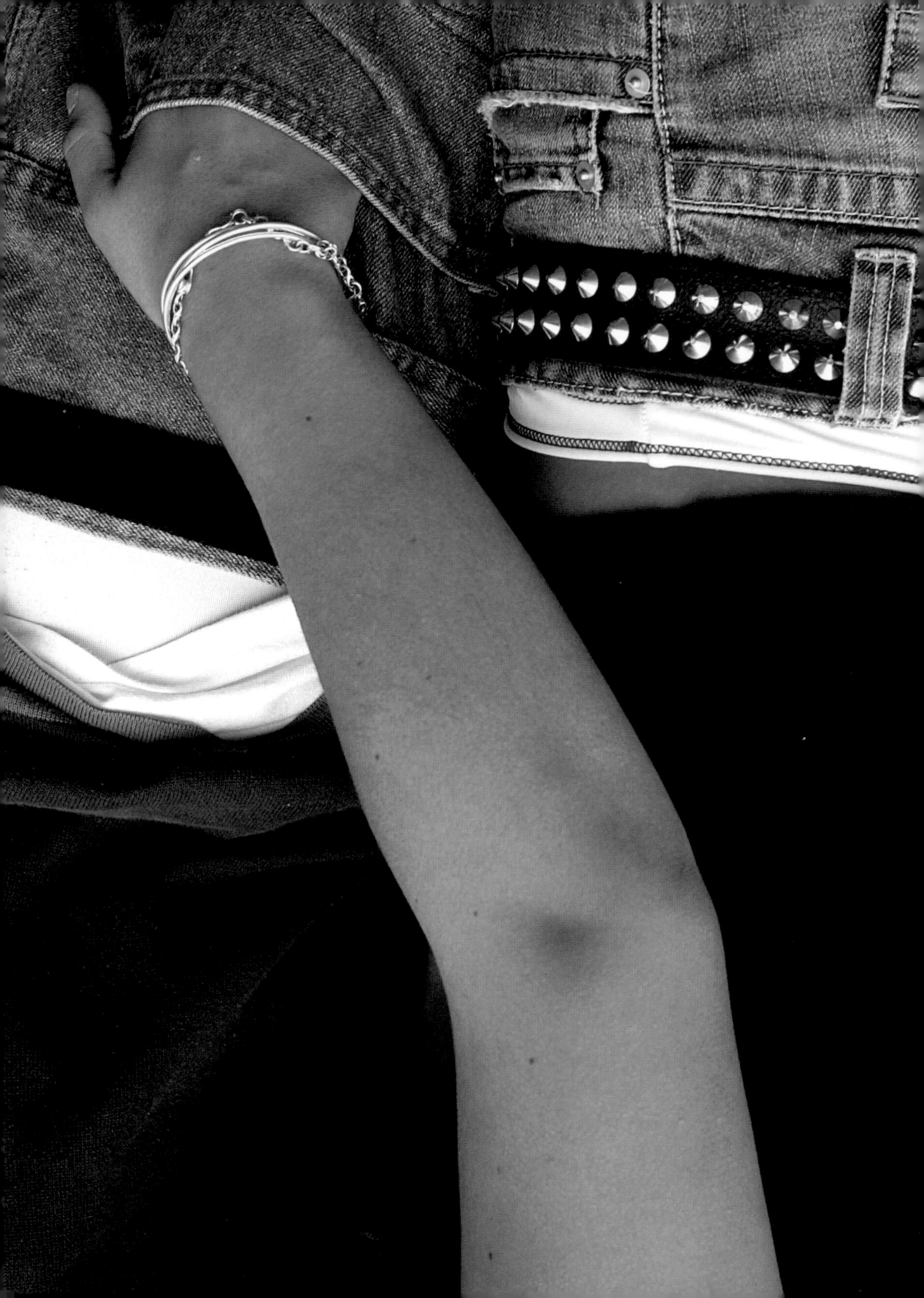

Knowing about your body is a really important part of enjoying sex and keeping safe and healthy. When it comes to sex, guys often only think about their dicks and balls, and maybe their bums. But what about your lips, tongues, hands, feet, arms, legs, head, ears, eyes, shoulders? All can provide you with a heap of pleasure! And what about your brain, mind, spirit or soul?

What all your bits are, how they work and how to look after them is also important to know as changes might be a clue that something's wrong. Knowing how your body looks, feels and smells is important if you want to be aware of any changes.

'HOW MUCH DO I KNOW ABOUT MY BODY?'

Pleasure and your body

Some people say your brain is the biggest sexual organ it decides what you find a turn-on. Others argue that your skin is the biggest sexual organ, as it provides the sensory information. Either way you look at it, the whole body is a sexual organ.

If your brain decides your feet are extremely erotic, you may get turned on if they get a bit of attention; but, if your brain thinks they're just for walking, all the attention in the world won't turn you on. Or, if your brain decides your bum is a sexual organ, you may feel great if it gets a bit of attention; but, if your brain thinks it's just for pooing, any attention to that area could leave you unimpressed.

Sometimes, if we're focused only on our dicks, we can be depriving or limiting our pleasure, and our partner's.

‘WHAT PARTS OF MY BODY TURN ME ON?’

FEELING HORNY?

So what actually happens when you get turned on? How does it feel in your body? How does it feel in your head or heart? One of the more obvious things is an erection, but a few more subtle things can happen as well. You can get goose bumps, the hair on your body can stand up on end, you can get flushed, your breathing pattern can change—sometimes faster and deeper, sometimes shallower—you might even forget to breathe.

In and out

Breathing plays a very important role in all aspects of life including sex. Try imagining your breath coming in through your nose, into your lungs then all the way down to your genitals—this can give you a stronger orgasm—make sure you are somewhere where it’s safe to make a bit of noise!

Some senses might be reduced; it might feel like the rest of the world outside your body disappears. Some senses might get enhanced; you might become more aware of everything that’s going on around you. Because sexuality is such an individual thing, not everyone reacts in the same way. Sometimes you can become scared or confused, feel frustrated or angry, get cold or shaky, feel like you’re outside of your body, or there may be no response at all.

If you are responding to sex in ways that you don’t like or that make you feel uncomfortable, it might be a sign that you’re not comfortable with the sex that you’re having or the relationship you’re in. You might want to get more information or support from one of the agencies or websites listed at the back of the book.

Your reproductive system or 'your bits'

Your reproductive organs are a lot more than your penis. A lot of your bits are inside your body. To give you a tour of 'the bits', we'll follow a sperm on its journey from creation in the testes to ejaculation from the penis.

ALL THIS AND PLEASURE!

Apart from reproduction, our bits can provide a whole lot of pleasure too . . . the prostate and the head of the penis are jam-packed with sensitive nerve endings . . . testes produce sperm and testosterone but they can also produce great feelings of pleasure when they are caressed, kissed or otherwise aroused!

The testes (balls, nuts, etc.) are a couple of oval-shaped glands whose main job is to produce sperm and testosterone. They hang inside the scrotum (ball bag, sack, etc.); hanging outside the body keeps them cool and healthy.

Testosterone is a male hormone (or androgen) that is responsible for turning us into guys—growth spurts and body changes during puberty are all kicked along by testosterone. Testosterone also plays a part in our sense of wellbeing, it affects our sex drive and can also help prevent osteoporosis . . . and it keeps the production of sperm up and running.

Sperm are the male reproductive cells . . . they are so small you can't see them with the naked eye but under a microscope they look a little bit like tadpoles—their tales help them to swim towards their goal—the egg.

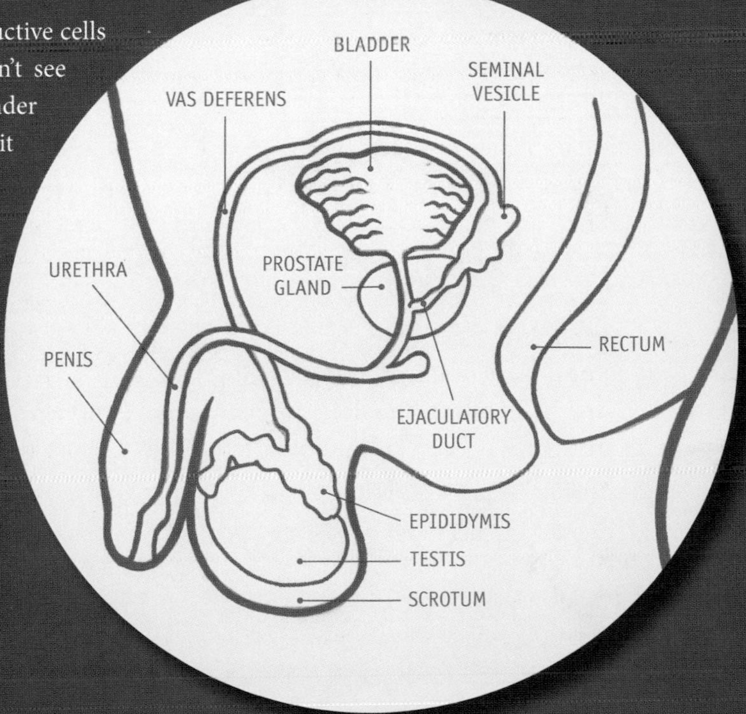

MITOCHANDRIAL SHEATH AROUND NECK REGION (provides energy)
MOVEMENT OF FIBRES IN TAIL CREATES MOTION
COVERING OF SPERM HEAD HELPS SPERM STICK TO AND PENETRATE EGG
SPERM HEAD CONTAINS TIGHTLY PACKED DNA (genetic material)

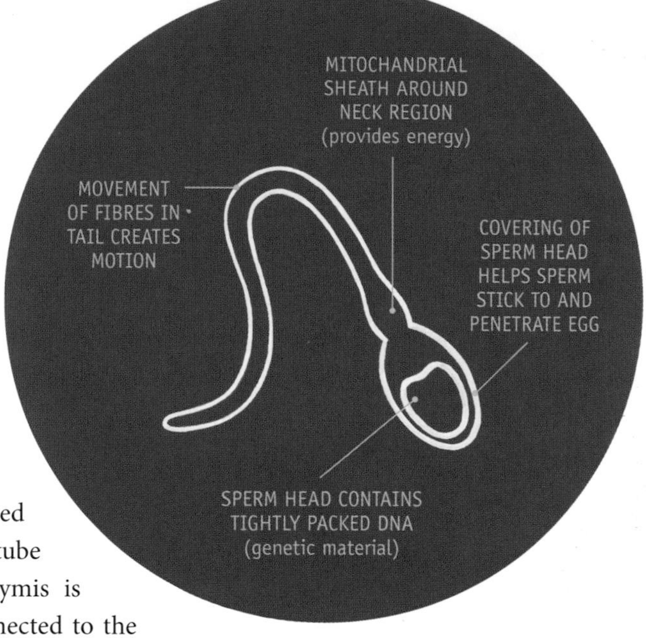

Once the sperm have been produced by the testes they move through a tube called the epididymis. The epididymis is 5 metres of coiled tube that is connected to the back of the testes. Here the sperm fully mature and gain the ability to swim.

When a guy reaches a sexual climax his brain sends messages through his nervous system that contract his pelvic muscles.

These contractions transport the sperm from the epididymis through a tube called the vas deferens. This tube transports the sperm up inside the body to the ejaculatory duct where it is mixed with a variety of fluids—all aimed at keeping the sperm nice and healthy.

These fluids are made by the Cowper's glands, the prostate gland and the seminal vesicle:

» The Cowper's glands produce a fluid that is released before ejaculation that neutralises any urine (which is too acidic for sperm) that may be left in the urethra (the tube that transports urine from the bladder and sperm, etc., along the length of the penis to exit at the tip).
» The prostate gland makes fluid that protects and feeds sperm (the vagina is not very 'sperm friendly'). This fluid surrounds the sperm and acts as a barrier.
» The fluid produced by the seminal vesicles is rich in a type of sugar that may be an energy source for sperm.

The sperm and supporting fluids are then moved along the urethra and out of the tip of the penis when the guy ejaculates.

If the guy ejaculates into a condom, or anywhere outside of a vagina, that's the end of the line for the sperm.

If the guy ejaculates inside a girl's vagina and there's no condom to catch the sperm they will try to swim up through the cervix. Some hormonal contraception prevents sperm from getting through the cervix by making the mucus covering the cervix thicker.

If the sperm make it through the cervix they head through the uterus and into the fallopian tubes looking for an egg to fertilise.

Some hormonal contraception prevents the release of an egg, but if there is one around, the sperm try to penetrate its outer layer to fertilise it.

Once the egg has been fertilised it begins to grow, moving down the fallopian tube and attaching itself to the wall of the uterus. Some hormonal contraception makes the lining of the uterus un-eggfriendly so an egg won't implant properly.

All going well, after approximately 40 weeks from conception (when the sperm fertilises the egg) a brand new human will be born into the world.

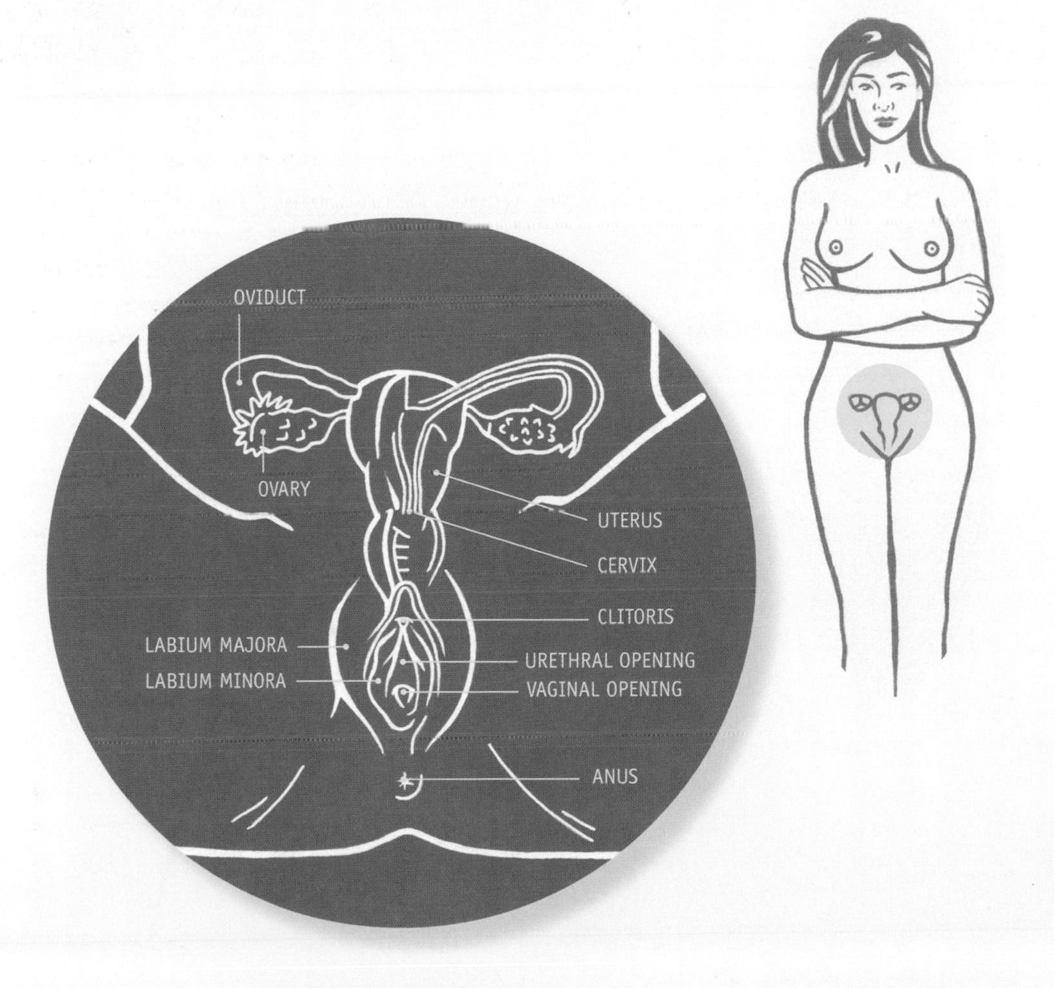

Testicular self-examination

The best time to check your testicles for lumps or bumps is after a warm shower or bath because they're hanging lower and are more sensitive to touch. One teste is usually bigger than the other and one often hangs lower—this is normal.

Check one teste at a time, roll it between your thumb and forefinger, looking for any changes—you're looking for a change in their size or shape. It's important to locate the epididymis at the back of the teste—lots of guys have mistaken this for a lump. It can also be a sign of something going on if your testes are painful or if they feel heavy, like they're dragging downwards. If you notice any changes get a doctor to check it out—most lumps are harmless cysts but the only way to be sure is to have them checked. The good news is that testicular cancer is one of the most easily treated forms of cancer. Guys are encouraged to start checking their testicles from age 15.

ORGASM AND EJACULATION

Guys often think of orgasm and ejaculation as the same thing, but they're not. Orgasm is a feeling of intense release when we reach the climax of our sexual excitement, while ejaculation is semen coming out of your penis.

While they often happen at the same time, some men are able to orgasm without ejaculating and some men are able to ejaculate without orgasm. Men often talk about orgasm without ejaculation as whole body orgasms! One method talks about training your body to orgasm without ejaculation by masturbating until you nearly ejaculate then stop for a while then do it again and again and eventually you may experience a whole body orgasm. It might not happen straight away and it might not happen all the time but it is *lots* of fun practising!

If you're interested in having sex with a girl, then you should flip your book and find out about their bodies and how they work . . . especially the clitoris and G-spot. We also talk more about women's bodies in Chapter 5, 'Doing It'.

DIFFERENT KINDS OF PENISES

One of the drawbacks of pornography is that we might get tricked into thinking a 'normal' penis is about 12 inches long, dead straight and always erect. Not so. There are many varieties of 'normal' when it comes to the penis.

Like people, penises come in many shapes, sizes and colours. And they're all normal. Penises can have bends in them, can be circumcised or still have their foreskin and they're all normal. They can be long, short, thick or thin, a penis can look different depending on how aroused you are—it could be soft and flaccid or hard and erect—it can even change colour!

Sometimes we can be worried about how our penis looks. Apart from the size thing, guys are often concerned by a bend or a curve in their penis.

Lots of guys have a curve in their penis—this might be harmless but it could be an early sign of Peyronies disease. This isn't a disease that you can catch; it's more like a callous on your foot. Skin cells harden like a scar and this skin doesn't stretch as much as the rest of the skin on the penis, so it causes the penis to bend. The good news is that there's treatment available.

If you're concerned about how your penis looks or works, contact one of the agencies or websites listed at the back of this book

What's normal about normal

There's a lot of pressure on people to appear 'normal'. This can stop us from talking openly or feeling okay about what we're doing (or not doing) sexually. **Remember, there is no such thing as normal.** Some things are more common, and you'll often hear about the average size of something, but this is because we live in a world of statistics where people are always reducing a large amount of information into a summary to get a handle on that information.

Unfortunately, this can cause a lot of fear, shame and guilt, especially when 'normal' or 'average' is attached to sex and sexuality. Whether you are talking about your body, your attitude towards sex, your fantasies or how you 'do it', fear that you are not like everyone else can isolate you and can sometimes make you think that you're a little weird . . . or a little 'not right'. 'I thought I was the only one' is a common statement.

Learning to love your body if it doesn't look or function the way you want it to can be extra hard. For instance, there's a lot of taboos around sexuality and disability—often people with disabilities aren't seen as sexual beings and are denied information about pleasure or keeping themselves safe. Or, if their sexuality is discussed, it's often in prying or disrespectful ways. Disability can be limiting but sex is un limited!

People are often afraid to talk about what turns them on for fear of being labelled, but a quick search on the web usually provides a community or forum for pretty much any passion.

Lots of gay guys talk about the energy it took to pretend to be heterosexual before they came out—sometimes that meant acting homophobic or having sex with a girl. When you realise that there're many different ways to be normal, you free up a lot of time and headspace that would otherwise be busy with 'appearing normal'—and realise that everyone is doing the same thing: trying to 'appear normal'.

'HOW DO I SEE MY SEXUALITY, AND HOW COMFORTABLE AM I WITH THAT?'

WHAT'S THE 'AVERAGE' PENIS SIZE?

Lots of guys worry about the size of their penis but, as you'll find out in the chapter 'Doing It', the female (and male) pleasure spots are well within reach of most penises. A lot of disappointment comes from measuring yourself against unrealistic benchmarks. For the most part, other erect penises we see are in porno movies, but these guys aren't of average size and they're definitely not selected for their acting abilities! And comparing flaccid (soft) penises isn't an accurate guide either. Flaccid penis size can change for a heap of reasons: like if it's cold or if you're scared, your penis can shrink slightly—this is self-protection, so don't worry it will come out again.

For those out there who want to know about average sizes, stats 'n' stuff, here we go:

» The average age of first sexual intercourse in Australia—16 years ('Australian study of health and relationships', 2002).
» The average penis size—14.75 to 15.75 centimetres. The biggest penis size—25 centimetres; the smallest 2.5 centimetres. Smaller than 2.5 centimetres is referred to as a 'micro penis' (Kinsey and Pomeroy reports).
» Average amount of cum—3 to 5 millilitres or about a teaspoon (*Urge*, 2002).
» Average amount of partners—in a survey of 34 000 internet users (in which half of the respondents were less than 25 years old), 4 per cent said they had slept with more than 100 people; 3 per cent said 50 to 100 people; 7 per cent said 21 to 30 people; 14 per cent said 11 to 20 people; and 20 per cent said 5 to 10 people (*The Penguin Atlas of Human Sexual Behaviour*, 2000).

Between you and me, that's all pretty average! I suggest you enjoy what you've got and what you're doing. If you aren't, get some support to make changes in your life to make it happen. Sex can be such a special thing, why try and make it average?

Why do guys have nipples?

When we were growing in our mother's uterus we all started off as basically genderless—yup, you read right—we weren't always guys! The nipples developed before the male hormone testosterone started turning us into guys.

More evidence of this is the fine line that goes from the back of your scrotum to underneath the tip of your penis—if you'd been born female that would have been the opening to your vagina!

SEX VERSUS GENDER

What's the difference between sex and gender? You could say that 'sex' is our biology or what's between our legs—whether we're a boy or a girl—but gender is about how we act—in a manly (masculine) or womanly (feminine) way. Both of these explanations can be limiting. Guys might not talk about feelings or emotions for fear of people labelling them as feminine, but your emotions are part of being a healthy human being.

We often think that people are either guys or girls, but it's not that simple. There are many examples of people that don't fit neatly into these boxes. Sometimes people are born with reproductive organs that aren't clearly just male or just female. You may have heard the term 'hermaphrodite', an old medical term for someone who is now more commonly seen as being intersexed (a new medical term). Another term you may have heard of is 'transgender'. The Seahorse Club of Victoria says it's 'an umbrella term used to describe all those whose gender identity is at odds with their biological sex' (http://home.vicnet.net.au/~seahorsc/glossary.html).

Apart from the more obvious physical differences, there are other ways men can be seen as different from women. One of these is brain function. No, one gender is not smarter than the other; the brain just works in different ways . . . we often process information differently. For example, some guys are better at estimating distance while some girls are better at talking about emotions or relationships. Having said that the opposite of that is true too, and then to further confuse things, our brains are changed by our experiences!!!

Another difference is in our chromosomes, which carry our genetic information in our cells. Guys are more often XY instead of XX . . . but not always.

Like I said, it's not that simple.

Unfortunately, we haven't got the space in this book to fully explore what all the differences are and mean, but in the resources section, 'Learn More', you'll find websites that will give you more information.

TRICKY QUESTIONS

Q **Do guys need to cum? If they don't ejaculate will their balls explode or turn blue?**

A No this is a myth, kind of—excess sperm is simply absorbed back into the body. A guy's testicles might feel a little achy after prolonged arousal without any release but it won't do him any harm to not ejaculate. I think it's an old tale designed to trick people into having sex . . . you can always masturbate to relieve the pressure.

Q **Is it healthy to be horny at a young age?**

A People are sexual beings from birth to death—I've raised sons and worked in an old folks' home so I've seen that that is true. Getting aroused or feeling horny can become associated with feelings apart from sexual stimulation—we might get erections when we feel safe and secure, when we're frightened, even in our sleep. If you're comfortable with it, feeling horny is healthy at any age.

Chapter 3

You, Your Mind and Sex

'If it works for you and that's how you get what you need, then that's cool.'

'Sex is whatever you want it to be, whatever you let it be.'

'If we are "in" our bodies then we can be "in" our sex.'

The connections between your mind and body are sometimes simple and obvious and sometimes complex and mystical. When it comes to sex, these connections can be all of these at once!

One of the biggest taboos in our society is our bodies. We cover them up, are taught not to touch them, and are taught to measure them against ideas of beauty that are often unreachable, and then feel bad about ourselves when we can't measure up—nasty! We can often highlight things we don't like about our bodies, but it can be harder to find the things that we do like.

Your body is the only one you've got so you might as well make friends with it. It can provide you with a lot of pleasure if you let it. So start noticing things YOU like about YOUR body. Feeling good about your body can be a key ingredient to feeling good about sex.

'IS IT OKAY TO HAVE EXPECTATIONS?'

Getting 'in touch' with your body

With the growing pains of puberty—unwanted erections, wet dreams and the awkwardness of growing into a bigger body—you can feel a bit detached from your body and may feel it's easier to ignore it all. But ignoring your body isn't treating yourself with respect and it isn't going to make you feel any better either.

Sometimes when you get turned on, you can get lost in fear, shame and guilt. All these things keep you from being 'in' your body. Let them go.

Think about how your body feels in a range of emotional states:

» How does your body feel when you are happy?
» How about when you're sad? Frightened? Confused? Scared? Horny? Or safe?
» How does your body feel when you masturbate—are you tense or relaxed?
» How does it feel emotionally when you have sex? Do you remember to breathe?

These feelings are all tools that you can use to be aware of what's going on inside and around you. Body awareness can help you stay safe and heighten your experience of pleasure. One of the things that can get you more in touch with your body is regular exercise. Try stretching, massage, meditation, yoga, tai chi, dancing and other sports. Eating and sleeping well keeps your body in good shape. All these things are the groundwork for great sex.

EXPLORING YOU, MENTALLY AND EMOTIONALLY . . .

Sexual identity is more than who you're attracted to. Your identity is influenced by your culture, your beliefs, values, attitudes, friends, family and experiences. Ask yourself these questions:

» Who are you attracted to?
» What are your expectations of sex?
» What do you expect from yourself?
» What are your expectations of a partner? Do you want to please your partner?
» What do you consider good sex?
» What are your personal boundaries? When do you say no?
» What's okay to do sexually? What's not?
» What's the stuff that's open to negotiation?

'WHAT NEGATIVE THOUGHTS DO I HAVE ABOUT MY BODY? HOW CAN I REPLACE THEM WITH SOME MORE POSITIVE THOUGHTS?'

Why do we think what we think?

The way we see the world can change over our lifetime. Changes in attitudes to children, racism, slavery, women's rights and homosexuality are all examples of this on a wider scale. When I was growing up, I thought sex was just about penetration. My experiences have shown me that sex is much more than that, so now I'm more focused on relating to and enjoying the person I'm with rather than just 'getting it in'.

Our beliefs guide our actions, and these actions have consequences that can change our beliefs. This is how we mature or develop as people. You can have experiences that encourage you to take risks. For example, you might believe that condoms are a waste of time, so you might have sex without them (action) and not catch a disease (consequence), which might reinforce your belief that they are a waste of time. But learning about the risks you take, or having an STI or pregnancy scare, might convince you otherwise.

Iceberg model AKA why do we do what we do?

People's behaviour is like an iceberg—you can only see 10 per cent of an iceberg but the other 90 per cent is under the water and remains unseen. Our behaviour is the 10 per cent that is seen—what is unseen are our beliefs, values, attitudes, past experiences and cultural upbringing. This all affects who we are and how we do what we do. This is why people are so different—we all have different experiences of life so we all have different experiences of sex and sexuality.

Knowing why you do what you do or being 'in' your mind can help you to act instead of reacting without thinking. Understanding that people act for a range of different reasons can help us develop empathy, which is useful if you want to be in a relationship with someone else.

'WHAT BELIEFS DO I HAVE ABOUT SEX?'

The hands-on approach!

Masturbation, wanking, spanking the monkey, self-love—whatever you call it, pleasuring yourself sexually can be a great way to find out what turns you on. It can also be a great way to relieve stress and help you get to sleep. If you're not into wanking, that's okay—no one should do anything sexual if they're not into it. But here's the good news . . . **wanking can be good for you!** Graham Giles, Director of Cancer Council Victoria's Cancer Epidemiology Centre, found that the more frequently men ejaculate, the less likely they are to develop prostate cancer. When they were in their 20s men who ejaculated seven or more times per week were a third less likely to develop aggressive prostate cancer ('Sexual factors and prostate cancer', *British Journal of Urology*, vol. 92, pp. 211–16.)

More than that, wanking is a great way to learn about your sexual self.

PLEASURE TIPS

I've put in some tips about pleasure because, well, they feel really good! Remember that wanking isn't just about your dick—explore and enjoy your whole body.

PLEASURE TIP 1 Water-based lube (lubricant) can make for a smoother, more enjoyable wank—it can get messy but it's heaps of fun and washes out in water.

PLEASURE TIP 2 A wank doesn't have to end with ejaculation—try touching other parts of your body after you've cum.

PLEASURE TIP 3 Cumming after an extended period of time can be more enjoyable than a daily dose.

PLEASURE TIP 4 A change is as good as a holiday. Using different materials, fantasies, hands, different temperatures (ice or warming lube, just don't use any of the lotions that heat up to fix sore muscles—ouch!) or different pressures can all provide different experiences—you're only limited by your imagination (and laws).

PLEASURE TIP 5 Make sure you've got plenty of time and privacy, that way you can let yourself go without worrying about someone barging in.

HYGIENE TIPS

Keeping your body clean and healthy is a top pleasure tip—and it shows you care about your body and you're considerate of your partner too. So here are my hints to keep you enjoying what you're doing.

HYGIENE TIP 1 Wash your hands before touching yourself.

HYGIENE TIP 2 Clean up after yourself. Some guys use a cum rag—this could be a towel, a bunch of tissues, a sock or a pair of boxers, some guys use their bedding: whatever method you use, remember to wash these regularly: old cum can get a bit stinky.

HYGIENE TIP 3 Some guys masturbate and cum in a condom, then tie it up and throw it away (don't flush it down the toilet—when the plumber unblocks the drain you'll hear about it).

HYGIENE TIP 4 Some guys cum on the floor—maybe volunteer to shampoo your carpet every now and again.

HYGIENE TIP 5 Some guys wank and cum in the bath or shower—remember to rinse afterwards.

HYGIENE TIP 6 Try and wash daily—even if it's a quick wash of your genitals it can help prevent unwanted smells.

Wanking: How much is too much?

Lots of guys ask how much is too much? Truth is, there's no set amount. A good guide is that if you're rubbed raw, or if it's getting in the way of everyday life, it might be a good idea to stop or slow down for a while. If you're masturbating more than you want to and want support, contact one of the agencies or websites listed in the resources section of this book, 'Learning More'.

The lowdown on porn

We talked a bit about porn and sex education in Chapter 1. Some people believe that porn can affect your attitudes towards or your expectations of sex, even the sex you have, for good and for worse. And what some people call 'pornography', others call 'art' or 'erotica'; it's a hotly debated subject.

Pictures of people having sex have been around for thousands of years. Now, with the internet and other digital media, it's readily available—statistically, the majority of downloads are porn-related. Because the internet and the use of mobile phones are so hard for governments to regulate, people of all ages have access to pretty much anything, including violent and degrading images . . . images that can give a dodgy sense of sex and sexuality. You do need to be aware that not all porn is legal.

THE PROS AND CONS OF PORN

I'm not here to say that porn is all good or all bad, but I will say some porn is definitely bad—anything that exploits people, anything that doesn't involve consent, anything using children or animals, is wrong. Watching violent or degrading porn can also have a damaging effect on your relationships, on the sex you have, and on your health and wellbeing.

Why some people hate porn:

» Porn can deeply offend some people.
» Porn can exploit women, those who work in the industry, as the roles they play are generally portrayed as submissive, existing only to please the guy.
» Porn can exploit men because their sexual needs, wants or insecurities are being used to make people rich.
» Porn exploits everyone by turning sex into a commodity.
» Porn can have a huge impact on a relationship. Sometimes partners can feel jealous, left out or second best to their partner's wish to watch porn.
» Some guys talk about being addicted to porn.
» Porn may present an unreal example of sex—this can put pressure on people to perform like a porn star or have sex they're not really comfortable with . . . and *you never see the bloopers.*

Why some people love porn:

» Porn can spice up your sex life if you are both into it.
» Porn can provide sexual pleasure.
» Porn can be seen as a sex education tool, helping you to understand ways of expressing your sexuality.
» You can't get pregnant or catch STIs from porn.
» Porn can provide an outlet for people whose sexuality is usually ignored by the mainstream media.
» Porn can provide opportunities to discuss what you do and don't like with your partner.

'WHAT DO I THINK ABOUT PORN?'

Porn is generally made by men for men, so it doesn't usually involve a lot of female ideas about sex and relationships. This can give a pretty unbalanced idea of what sex is all about—and it can be limiting if you want to be sexual with a girl and give her pleasure.

You can flip your book to see what *Sexpectations Girl* thinks about pornography. A good source of information about what girls think is the magazines they read—plenty of them have articles about sex and relationships. And don't flick past articles about abusive relationships or unwanted sex—it's a good way to learn what not to do. But if you can talk to your partner openly and honestly about sex, you might as well go straight to the source.

Sexting—porn or a bit of fun?

Lots of couples send each other sexy text or picture messages. Some people see this as a bit of fun, but others say that it's pornography. If the person in the picture is under 18 you may be charged with producing or distributing child pornography—a label that can follow you for the rest of your life. With all digital media you risk your image being used in ways that you might not be able to control—once it's out there it's out of your hands.

If you feel like you're using porn in a positive, respectful way, that's cool. But if you're concerned about your use of porn and want support, contact one of the agencies or websites listed in the resources section of this book.

TRICKY QUESTIONS

Q **How do you know if porn is good or bad?**

A When it comes to art, everyone has different ideas of what's good and bad but, when it comes to porn, a good guide is pleasure. Do the people involved look like they really want to be doing what they're doing? Do they look like they're really enjoying it? Are they treating each other with respect? Is it clear that they are all consenting to what's going on? If so, then you've possibly got some positive respectful entertainment going on.

If it looks like they're off their face or that they're putting up with stuff they're not really okay with or if consent isn't being freely given, then you've got to ask yourself what's going on. Do I really want to get off on other people's misery and vulnerability?

Q **What if my partner doesn't like my sex rules?**

A You have to weigh up what's more important to you—being in the relationship or having all of your sex rules met. It might be useful to think about which sex rules you're talking about. Is it some rules in particular or all of them? Are they your bottom-line sex rules or ones that are open to negotiation?

If all of your rules are being ignored it can be really difficult, if not impossible, to maintain a healthy relationship. Communication and negotiation are essential to getting our needs met in a relationship. If your partner and your rules don't mix, then it might be better to end the relationship and find a partner who you will be more sexually compatible with.

Q **My friend just told me he is gay. I want to support him, so what can I do to help?**

A Keeping the friendship going is a great start.

Being gay doesn't necessarily mean they'll need any kind of support, but if it looks like your friend is having a hard time, the best way to support anyone with anything is to ask them how you can help. It can be too easy to go ahead with what we think should happen rather than listen to what they actually want to happen. Most importantly, it's up to them to decide if and how they come out to other people. If they don't want to let anyone know, make sure you don't accidentally 'out' them.

They might be keen to talk about their sexual identity, but they might also want to talk about what's happening this weekend. Coming out can be a big thing but it's important to remember all the other things that go into your friendship and keep nurturing those.

Chapter 4

The First Time—Lust, Love 'n' All That

'It didn't help that I was drunk.'

'We'd been together for ages.
We'd talked about sex.
When we got together it was a natural
progression of exploring each other.'

FIRST SEXUAL EXPERIENCES ARE OFTEN MIXED BAGS—there can be the thrill of pleasure and being with someone, or the relief of finally 'doing it' mixed with the disappointment or embarrassment of failed expectations, or the confusion or fear of unwanted sex.

Sometimes first sexual experiences can be sex games with friends. Lots of guys I've talked with have had great shame because their first sexual experiences have been with other guys—it could have been masturbating together or penis sword fights in the shower. This is natural exploration of sexuality—it's just when we add homophobia (fear/hatred of people who are same-sex attracted) that it can become something shameful.

The following quotes are from real guys about their first time:

'The first time I had sex I very nearly didn't . . . I didn't want to make the first move—it must have been really frustrating for her. She'd made it really clear that she wanted to have sex with me and here I was messing about, trying to be really casual about it all. Then it all happened . . . I'd seen plenty of naked bodies but here was someone that wanted me to touch them, and wanted to touch me. It was awesome . . . feeling skin on skin, the warmth of another human. I didn't really know what to do so I just went through all the motions that I'd seen in movies. It didn't last very long and after it was all over, I just wanted her to leave before my folks came home. I knew it was not the way to go, but I wanted to be alone—it was confusing. I'd wanted to have sex for ages, now I had the chance and all I wanted was for her to go. For my part there wasn't any real loving there, just a warm body to be with. I think she wanted more—to be held and cared for but I just didn't know how to do it.'

'I lost my virginity at a crazy house party. Everyone was off their face. I was kissing and cuddling a good friend then we went out into the backyard and laid down on the grass. She started going down on me and it was f%#ing great—except I really needed to piss. After a while I couldn't stand it any longer so I went for a piss then came back—she wouldn't suck me anymore, but we started playing with each other again and she jumped on top of me. We found out later that most of the party had been watching us—it was kind of embarrassing.'*

'The first time I had sex, my mates arranged a prostitute for my 18th birthday. It was great and terrifying. I was scared I'd catch AIDS or that she'd be really horrible and smelly. It turned out she looked like a businesswoman and was full-on with the safe-sex stuff. She taught me more about sex in an hour than I'd learned in 12 years of school. She taught me about respect and consent and how to go slow. She didn't care that I came really quickly. She was very gentle.'

'The first time I had sex was great and horrible . . . I had a crush on this girl who lived nearby. We started talking one day and ended up back at her place, just sitting on her bed, then all of a sudden she was all over me—which sounds good but I was hoping to go a bit slower—it was kinda scary. After I came, she got up and said I had to go because her boyfriend was coming round soon. I was devastated. I had all these romantic ideas of love and stuff. I couldn't talk to my mates 'cos they would've paid me out—and besides, they thought I was a legend for having sex.'

'The first time I had sex was with a friend of mine didn't want me to go off to college a virgin. Then I went to college and discovered other guys—so that's another first right there.'

'I'm not sure if it counts, but the first time I was inside another person I was really drunk and had trouble getting a hard-on. Technically speaking, I was inside of her but I didn't cum and we didn't try too long. We ended up trying again and we've been together for four years now. She still reminds me—drunken sex sucks.'

'I've had so many first times—the first time with someone new is always special, and scary. I reckon the first time shouldn't count—there's always too much pressure. You've gotta have sex at least three times before you can judge if you're sexually compatible with someone.'

'First time I was drunk and I couldn't find where to put it. Obviously, I was teased by my mates—we were playing mini golf and they were saying, "See if you can get it in the hole this time!" Next time I was sober and everything went okay. It didn't help that I was drunk the first time.'

'The first time I had sex, it blew my mind but I couldn't boast to anyone, I had to be casual about it all—I'd pretended to have sex ages before that.'

'HOW DO YOU WANT YOUR FIRST TIME TO BE OR HOW DO YOU WANT YOUR NEXT TIME TO BE?'

Virginity and losing it

What is virginity? A very simple way of looking at it is that you're a virgin if you haven't had sex with anyone. Losing your virginity means having sex with someone for the first time. But it can be a little more complicated.

Some people see sex as having penetrative, penis-in-vagina sex. But oral sex is sex, so does that mean you've lost your virginity if you've given or received head? And what about anal sex? Some cultures practise anal sex as a way of protecting virginity, believing that only penis–vagina sex means losing your virginity. What if you only have sex with guys and your penis never goes anywhere near a vagina—ever?

And what about sexual assault—does that count? Lots of people see sexual assault as being an abuse of power, they don't see it as sex at all, so that might not count as losing your virginity.

So maybe there're many different types of virginity—oral, anal, vaginal, gay, heterosexual. How you see your own virginity is the most important definition.

Some religions see virginity as special: a gift from God to be saved until marriage. This is so important in some cultures that a new bride is expected to bleed during sex on the wedding night as a sign that she was a virgin (the bleeding is meant to happen because the hymen, a layer of skin that partially covers the vagina, is broken by the husband's penis). Sometimes proof of this is required by the family in the form of a bloodied sheet. However, the hymen can be broken by lots of other activities—like riding a horse or strenuous exercise—so it's not a very good tool for judging virginity. It's a bit of a double standard too, as there's not much pressure to prove that the guy was a virgin.

For lots of people virginity is very important—they've decided to wait until they meet the right person or they're married. But, for lots of other people, virginity doesn't matter at all—they can't wait to lose it and start their exploration of sex.

There's so much importance placed on losing your virginity, and some people expect their world to change forever and are disappointed that no one even notices. It can be especially hard if your partner doesn't even notice.

If you're going to go for it . . .

You might want to remember that you'll never have your first time again. Lots of people report feeling pretty let down by their first sexual experience. There's so much pressure that you can end up having a pretty average time—it might be embarrassing, boring or even scary. First-time sex might even be painful—you are expecting your body to do something it hasn't done before. One of the guys I interviewed was surprised at the amount of energy it took to have sex: 'No one ever suggested I do warm-up stretches or anything like that.'

Alcohol is often associated with first-time sex—you may use it to relax or lower your inhibitions, but you may also make choices you wouldn't usually make. Alcohol might influence your choice about who you have sex with, the precautions you take (think condoms) or your ability to make sure you're getting consent—if someone is too trashed to say no, they're also too trashed to say yes. If you really want to have sex with someone but they're under the influence of drugs or alcohol, wait until they've straightened out and make sure they really do want to have sex with you.

Making sure that your partner wants to have sex with you is a must. If they don't, chill out—*never* try and trick, force or manipulate anyone into anything.

MAKING THE FIRST TIME GOOD

The good news is some people have really good first-time sex experiences. So what makes the difference?

Your expectations of first-time sex can greatly influence your experience. Here's what a few guys had to say about their expectations of their first sexual encounter:

- 'I will know what to do.'
- 'It will be pleasurable—feel good.'
- 'I'll be able to pleasure my partner.'
- 'It will be with someone I love.'
- 'My partner will want to have sex with me.'

Some of those responses are a pretty big ask for something the first time round.

'WHAT DO I EXPECT THE FIRST TIME?'

After the first time

If you've already had first-time sex and it wasn't the best, don't give yourself a hard time—use it as a learning experience. What wasn't so good about it? How can you make it better next time?

Sex is like any other activity—we all need practice and some help to get it right.

KNOWING ABOUT SEX CAN HELP

» Know about the risks you're taking—what are the consequences if something goes wrong?
» Know how to stay safe—sex is a lot more fun if you don't have to worry about pregnancy or STIs.
» Trust the person you're with—trust that they won't harm you.

HAVE REALISTIC EXPECTATIONS

» Don't expect fireworks.
» Don't expect that you'll both know what to do—you're learning.
» Expect to be treated with respect.

BE PREPARED

» Have somewhere safe to do it.
» Make sure you have privacy.
» Have plenty of time.
» Do plenty of talking—so you're both clear about what's going on.

A good relationship . . . and great sex

'Relationships—it's what life's all about . . . Relating to yourself, relating to the people around you, relating to the world in general.'

'Relating is foreplay. Foreplay doesn't last for ten or fifteen minutes—it's all day, all week, all year. It starts the moment you meet, it's how you look at each other, it's how you treat each other. You can't treat someone like shit all day then snuggle up a bit and expect sex.'

Sex and being in a relationship often go hand in hand. What words do you use for someone you're with—'girlfriend', 'lover', 'partner', 'your other half'? Or are you 'seeing someone', 'having a thing with them' or are they 'friends with benefits'? Maybe you don't even want to label what's going on—it just *is*. Words are tricky.

Knowing what you want from a relationship can help you to find someone who fits with your

sex expectations. Of course, there are no guarantees—what you want today could be different from what you will want later on, the same goes for your partner.

If you want just sex from a relationship, that's okay too, but be honest with the other person about it. There's no guarantee that honesty will get you what you want, but at least you won't have to pretend or lie— and you can look at yourself in the mirror; self-respect is a good thing. Your honesty might even make you some good friends. You'll definitely keep more *real* friends that way.

What I hear a lot of young people saying is that they want a safe, satisfying relationship with someone they love and trust and who loves and trusts them . . . oh, and great sex! People often get confused between love and sex. Sometimes people use love to get sex or sex to get love. When you do this, you can often end up feeling a bit let down or used.

'HAVE I BEEN HONEST WITH MY PARTNER ABOUT WHAT I WANT?'

RELATIONSHIP EXPECTATIONS

Like people, relationships come in all shapes and sizes. It's up to you and your partner to make the rules. Some realistic expectations could be:

- that you will be treated with respect and cared for
- that you will feel safe and be safe
- that there'll be ups and downs
- that it will be hard work every now and again.

Some unrealistic expectations are:

- that one person will be everything—lover, parent, therapist, conscience (making them responsible for your behaviour)
- that a relationship will fulfil all your needs and fix all your problems
- that true love runs smoothly
- that if they love you, they'll put up with anything you do
- that you'll know what your partner is thinking and they'll know what you're thinking
- that sex will fix an unhealthy relationship.

'AM I BEING REALISTIC ABOUT MY SEX EXPECTATIONS IN MY RELATIONSHIP?'

What's lust got to do with it?

Lust adds a whole other level of confusion. Your body can seem out of control with desire for someone, yet when you think about it, you might not even like them. They might really annoy you but you might still want to have sex with them—confusing, hey? Everyone knows that drugs and alcohol can affect the choices you make—but did you know that being horny can affect your judgement too ?

Lust is all about the body—physical urges. Love goes a little deeper—it's all about the heart, mind and soul connections. But sometimes the physical urges are so strong that you can create the heart, mind and soul connections in your head—like falling in love with someone you've never met.

INTIMACY AND SEX AREN'T THE SAME THING

Lots of guys see sex as a way of being intimate with their partner. For lots of guys I've talked with, this is the only way they can be intimate with their partner. This is a common complaint from heterosexual girls—every time they want to have a cuddle, their boyfriend gets the idea that they want sex. In this situation they are both wanting intimacy, but a lack of communication ends up in misunderstandings and resentment.

Sometimes being intimate means being vulnerable. Being open and honest with someone else means that you care about them. Intimacy is learned: if we've learned that vulnerability and intimacy are signs of weakness it can be hard to be intimate with someone we want to be close with. If people have taken advantage of our vulnerability previously it can be really hard to open up and risk getting hurt again, but the risk of not opening up is that we never let anyone get really close to us.

Unfortunately, guys are often taught to be tough, and to be tough sometimes means rejecting any forms of intimacy. Quite often, if guys show they care about something, this can be used against them. Have you ever said 'I don't care' about something when you really did? This can be a good way of protecting yourself, but it can also keep you from being close to other people.

Being intimate means being brave. Taking a chance that the person you're with won't use your vulnerability against you. I won't lie to you, it can be really scary and sometimes people will abuse that trust, but the pay-off can be a stronger relationship.

‘WHAT HAVE I LEARNED ABOUT INTIMACY AND BEING VULNERABLE?

‘Boys and men learn very early to discount their own emotional needs, which then makes it difficult to recognize or respond to the needs of others.’

(Norman Dean Radican, ‘Men and sex and fear and intimacy’, in *On the Level*, vol. 3, no. 4, 1995, pp. 36–8)

How to be intimate without having sex

If your partner doesn't want sex, then you have to respect that. You can still enjoy each other's company in an intimate way by:

» kissing and cuddling each other
» giving each other a massage
» cooking a meal together
» talking about each other's day
» sharing your secrets
» making plans to do things
» going for a walk, swim, etc.
» sharing a bath—get some candles and essential oils
» leaving love notes where only they can find them
» sending a personal email or text—although be aware that this can get messy as you can't guarantee who'll see it
» going camping.

Lots of these things could lead to sex but if you expect or push for sex instead of enjoying being close to your partner, their trust in you will go out the window as your efforts might be seen as a form of coercion.

Making the right moves

Being aware of your own body is a good start to picking up other people's body language. How do you stand when you're interested in someone? How about when someone makes you feel uncomfortable? Do you cross your arms or sit away from them?

There are some clues to knowing if someone's interested in you:

- They make eye contact—this can be difficult to do and it shows interest and openness. Try not to stare, though, it's scary.
- They play with their hair or check their appearance.
- They move towards you.
- Their feet are pointed at you.
- They lean forward towards you.
- Their body is open to you—no crossed arms or legs, these act as barriers.
- They mirror you by copying your movements—a flick of the hair, or sitting a certain way.
- They touch you—a pat on the arm or a gentle push could be a good sign.

CURSE OF THE FRIENDLY FLIRTER

Flirting is natural human behaviour—it doesn't always mean we want to have sex with the person we're flirting with. Sometimes it's just nice to be noticed by someone. What some people see as flirting, some see as simply being nice, while other people see it as being disrespectful or even cheating. So it's up to you and your partner to work these things out.

I know a few people who are really outgoing and friendly—they do all of the things mentioned above and the fact is they are interested, but not necessarily as partners or lovers. They're just genuinely interested in people. This can lead to a lot of confusion and heaps of guys (including myself) can get the impression that they were looking for more.

So how do you tell the difference? The simple answer is to just ask. You might not want to hear the answer but it could be better than struggling on in the dark. Or you could bring up the curse of the friendly flirter—ask if they are a sufferer. At least you'll get a laugh, at best you'll be able to talk about what's going on for you and get some clarity either way.

'WHAT DO YOU THINK ABOUT FLIRTING THAT DOESN'T LEAD TO SEX?'

Relationships—so many styles to choose from!

Sexual relationships can be one-night stands or long term, they can be just about sex or love or both, they can have all the wonderful highs and terrible lows. They can be healthy and fulfilling and they can be abusive and destructive, and they can be just plain confusing. So what are the possibilities?

ONE-NIGHT STANDS

You meet someone, you like them, they like you, and you both agree to have sex that night. Be sure you want to. Be really clear about what's going on and make sure you are both consenting to sex. One-night stands can be fun or they can be a nightmare just waiting to happen, particularly if you've been drinking. Be aware of the following:

- Remember condoms, condoms, CONDOMS (and lots of water-based lube).
- Are they old enough? Just because someone's in a pub or club it doesn't mean they're over 18 years old.
- Make sure you have some way to get home.
- If possible, tell a friend where you're going.
- If you're going to stay at their place or they're going to stay at yours, be prepared for awkwardness in the morning—and morning-after breath.
- Remember that sex in public places is illegal.
- Remember emergency contraception.

FRIENDS WITH BENEFITS

Sometimes a friendship can become sexual—it doesn't have to turn into a boyfriend/girlfriend thing. Sex with a friend can be very intimate as you already know and like the other person. But there can be a few drawbacks: one person might want more than sex and friendship; you might lose the friendship.

Communication is vital. Be up-front with the person involved. Be clear about what's going on. You might want to discuss what would happen if one of you finds a partner. Friends with benefits can still become jealous.

OPEN RELATIONSHIPS

Some people have 'open relationships', where they can have sex with other people. Some people have open relationships where they can fall in love with someone else too. Whether it's just sex, or love too, open relationships can raise a few extra issues:

- Trust—You must trust that your partner won't do anything to harm you or the relationship. That could mean making sure they only have safer sex, or stick to any rules or boundaries that you've agreed on.
- Consent—Everyone involved has to be okay with what's going on. If someone is just doing it to please their partner, sooner or later they're probably going to feel used, jealous or bitter.
- Communication—Talk honestly about your needs and desires. Feel safe to say stop at anytime.
- Boundaries—Specify what's okay to do outside of the relationship and what's not.
- Some people use condoms and dams as an emotional barrier as well as a barrier to STIs and sperm.

SAME-SEX RELATIONSHIPS

Sometimes labels get in the way—we often use the term same-sex attraction to get away from the idea that a label defines what you do; for example, some guys who have sex with other guys don't see themselves as bisexual or homosexual yet they have some same-sex attraction.

Same-sex attraction is a natural part of human sexual diversity. Homosexuality has been around in every culture throughout history, but it hasn't always been an issue like it seems to be today.

Same-sex relationships are pretty much the same as opposite-sex relationships; however, there is the added pressure of homophobia. Imagine if you couldn't show your love in public for fear of harassment, discrimination and violence. Many gay people move to escape this abuse. Unfortunately, this separates them from the support of their family and community, which can create even more pressure.

Some people look for causes of homosexuality as if same-sex attraction isn't natural (think straight versus bent). They claim it's because of genes or hormones or trauma or having two dads or no dads, etc. I think this is a waste of time, and we'd be better off looking for causes of homophobia because this is where the real problem lies. Just to be clear, there has been no conclusive proof about what causes homosexuality. Hate and fear get in the way of good sex and safe, happy communities.

'Once young people reframed their experiences of homophobia as an issue of bullying and not of truths about themselves, they were more likely to feel better about being same-sex attracted.'

Lynne Hillier et al., *Writing Themselves in Again (A report on the health of same-sex-attracted young people)*, 2005

But guys do have long-term, successful, happy, healthy relationships with other guys. As my gran said, 'It doesn't matter if it's a man or a woman—love is love.' This was from a 96-year-old, hard-core, Scottish fisherwoman—I guess you learn a few things in 96 years! I learned not to assume that oldies knew nothing about same-sex love . . . and lots of young uns know it too . . .

'MY DAD THINKS I ROCK COZ I DON'T HATE DUDES THAT DIG THE COCK.'

From Facebook entry of interviewee

CROSS-CULTURAL RELATIONSHIPS

Attitudes to sex, love and relationships are different around the world. If your partner comes from another culture, communication can be even more important. Having an understanding of your partner's cultural norms (what's okay and what's not) can prevent embarrassment or awkwardness. In some cultures, however, talking about sex, especially with someone from the opposite sex can be very shameful. A good place to start is to ask your partner what stuff is okay to talk about.

Try not to force your cultural norms onto them. Learn from each other. Like any relationship, if it's going to work, it's got to work for both of you.

ONLINE SEX

Online chat rooms and dating services can bring the world to your computer. You can be intimate with people you'll never meet. Body language goes out the window—replaced with typing skills and Photoshop.

The internet has created an online community where people can explore their sexuality, even their gender. But just as this creates some safety, it also creates some dangers—remember, that 14 year old from Denmark could be a 40 year old from around the corner.

Always protect yourself. If you put a digital image out there, it is out of your control. You might just be sending it to your partner's phone but you never know who's going to look at it. Once it's been sent, it could end up anywhere thanks to the ease of information sharing. And don't give out your details, whether it's your home address, phone number, where you go to school or your bank details (or your parents' bank details). These can be used to locate you—online predators are skilled at taking advantage.

If you meet someone online and agree to meet them in person, make it a public place and take along a friend. It's not always easy to take a friend if you're meeting someone but it can make it a little more relaxed and a lot safer. At the very least let someone know where you're going and who you're going to meet—maybe get them to give you a call to make sure everything is going okay by arranging a codeword to alert them if you're feeling unsafe.

If you have any concerns, contact the Australian Communications and Media Authority at www.acma.gov.au/hotline or Net Alert at www.australia.gov.au/netalert.

RELATIONSHIPS WITHOUT SEX

I'm guessing you're already having lots of relationships without sex—teachers, friends, work mates—but it's also possible to be with a partner and not have sex. People abstain from sex for many reasons. Lots of religions don't agree with sex before marriage; sex might go against their personal beliefs; or they might just be waiting to be absolutely sure that they want to have sex—there's no use-by date when it comes to sex.

Just because someone doesn't have sex it doesn't mean they aren't sexual beings—they may still have sexual feelings, they just don't act on them. It's important to acknowledge and respect the discipline that this takes.

AGE GAPS

Some of the guys I've talked with had learned about sex through older partners—but this rarely went on to become anything more. It seems that when it comes to relationships, especially when you're in your teens, too much of an age gap can get in the way of a healthy relationship. It could be that your interests are too different or the older person may use their experience of the world to manipulate the younger person.

What about you? Would you have a relationship with someone older than you? How old is too old? What if they were younger? How young is too young?

Remember age of consent: what's the age of consent to sexual intercourse where you live? Check out the map in the girls' section on page 13. Remember, too, that if you're under the age of consent, even if you want to have sex with an older man or an older woman, it's still against the law and the adult is still 100 per cent responsible for anything that happens.

THREESOMES AND MORESOMES

If one of your fantasies is involving more than two people in sex, you might want to do a fair bit of thinking before you give it a try in reality. When you bring in other people, you involve all of their sexpectations too. Remember, it might be a fantasy but you're interacting with real people with real feelings.

You might want to make some boundaries or rules about what's going to go on—it's just like setting boundaries as a couple but with extra people. Of course, one of those rules might be that there are no rules!

Some people who have had experience with group sex suggest making sure that no one is left out and that everyone practises safer sex. So if you're going to have sex with multiple partners, change condoms when swapping partners.

Making sure that everyone really wants to go ahead with it is essential. As with any sexual activity, if someone is being manipulated into it or they're just doing it to please their partner, they will probably end up feeling used, jealous or angry.

Violence and abuse: never

Whatever style of relationship you are in, a healthy relationship never involves violence or abuse.

TRICKY QUESTIONS

Q What can you do with your lover that doesn't cost too much money?

A Okay, this is where the hippy in me comes out: nature's for free—a walk in the park, by a river or on the beach can be a great no pressure (cheap) date. How about a home-cooked meal—you could cook together. You could exercise or create art together. Trading massages is a really healthy way to nurture each other. What about the free stuff around you? Local councils often put on free or low-cost events. Stay in—go through each other's music collection. Go out—local music is often free entry; keep an eye on the local music press to see what's going on. Going op-shopping together can be a heap of fun. If you've got a bike you could head off together for a trek or a quick spin . . . also explore each other's fantasies, brains, minds, lives, bodies, etc.

Q How can I show respect?

A It can be hard to show respect if we've not seen much of it growing up. Sometimes we can get confused between fear and respect. You can show respect by not betraying secrets, by respecting your partner's boundaries, by listening to what they're saying, by fighting fair when you're in conflict with your partner. You don't have to always agree, but you do always have to respect each other's right to an opinion. Admit when you are wrong. Don't abuse your power over others. Respect yourself.

Q Can you be in love with two people at the same time?

A Quick answer is yes—but that doesn't make it any easier. We're often taught that we'll have only one true love and that anyone else is a threat to that love.

Sometimes people arrange their relationship to accommodate more than one lover but this takes a lot of commitment to the relationship and a lot of negotiation. Working out the rules for two people is hard enough—when you include more people you include their sex rules too. Loving more than one person can be a real threat to a partner's sense of security. You're not responsible for their feelings, but how you show your love for them and, more importantly, how you show your love for the other person can greatly impact on their sense of wellbeing.

Chapter 5

Doing It

'Listen to who you're with, listen to how they want it to happen. If it feels better for them, chances are it will feel better for you.'

'Consent is the sexiest. Knowing that someone really wants to do what you really want to do—pure gold!'

'My partner really likes repetition—staying with the one move—it lets her build up to a killer orgasm.'

'Sex tips—I could give you plenty of them, but I'm not about to give away my styles or my skills.'

One of the big pressures for guys is to be a legend in the sack. It might be our first time but we often expect fireworks and may feel let down if they don't go off. So how do you get competent and confident about sex?

It might be useful to think about competence in another area—for example, riding a bike. You don't jump on and expect to ride confidently straight away. We might fluke a good ride here and there, but generally we don't head straight to the ramps. So how do we learn?

You've been subconsciously learning since you became aware that people rode bikes. You've seen that people sit on the seat and make the pedals go round and round. It's the same with sex (and relationships)—you've been subconsciously learning since you found out about it.

Often we'll give ourselves a hard time if we screw it up. But, as one of the guys I interviewed said, 'It's not screwing up, it's learning'—what a great attitude. If you can admit that you're learning, then you'll open yourself up to new information. But if you always pretend to be an expert, you've got nowhere to go. The reality of sex and sexuality is that there's always more to learn, practise . . . and enjoy !

'DO MY FEARS STOP ME FROM FEELING COMFORTABLE ABOUT SEX?'

Technique—ins and outs and ups and downs

There're infinite ways to be sexual, but it's up to you and your partner to discover what works best for you. Sometimes a quickie can be really intense for both parties—ensure consent, get naked (or nearly naked), then eat each other alive is about all the technique required. But you might want to put in a little more effort.

Here're some suggestions to help get you started . . .

KISSING

Kissing is important, that's all I've got to say. *Sexpectations Girl* has some great info on kissing so I won't double up—flip your book to find out more.

TOUCHING

We all have different experiences of touch. For example, touch might have been used against you in violent or abusive ways, so being close with someone, touching someone or having them touch you can be pretty scary. Remember safety is the key.

Sometimes we'll be tempted to behave like an octopus—hands and tongues everywhere at

once. Some people might like this but many prefer sensual, focused caring, gentle touch and this can change from moment to moment. Really pay attention to the body part you're touching—focus your love or your sexual energy. Sometimes our partners might get over-stimulated or go numb—take a break or try something different.

Ask your partner how they like to be touched. They may want to show you or guide your fingers. Never be afraid to ask for help—and don't refuse any feedback.

Don't head straight for their genitals. Start softly, slowly—massage their back or feet, rub their arms or legs, a head massage feels great. At this stage, it's all about teasing and pleasing, feeling good and getting in touch with pleasure.

Unfortunately, there's no recipe-style time line (massage 10 minutes, masturbation 10 minutes, oral 10 minutes), so you'll have to be guided by your partner or trust your instincts about when to move on. Remember, there's no rush—rushing gets you nowhere fast.

Rubbing nipples is *not* like popping a pimple—be gentle. Trace your finger around their breast, take a nipple between your thumb and first finger. Make sure you pay attention to both breasts, no one wants to be left out. Kissing and sucking can be nice, some people like gentle biting.

Gentle kisses can be an interesting way to make your way around your partner's body.

FOREPLAY

Some people look at foreplay as a warm-up to 'real' sex so they might not pay much attention to it—they see it as something to rush through. Some people don't believe in the term foreplay at all—they say it's all sex. A friend of mine once said, 'The best lover I ever had wouldn't put his penis near me until I'd come at least once'—now that's a great attitude to foreplay.

Everyone has different takes on what foreplay is, but generally it includes some of the things we're talking about here—kissing, touching, maybe oral sex. Foreplay is really important to girls; flip your book and check out what they think about it.

If you treat foreplay as real sex and get enjoyment out of giving and receiving, it becomes much more interesting and pleasurable. Foreplay is a good way to work out how your partner is feeling about having sex. It's also great for getting to know each other's bodies and for making you both feel comfortable, which can lead to fantastic sex.

'DO I KNOW WHAT MY PARTNER LIKES WHEN IT COMES TO FOREPLAY?'

A quick lesson on girls' bodies

Before we go any further, we need to talk about girls' genitals. After all, if you're going to get intimate with these body bits, you better know something about them. Firstly, if you haven't already done it, flip your book and take a look at the descriptions in the girls' section. We won't be going over the basic stuff again; here, we're talking about those bits and how to pleasure them.

We often refer to all of a girl's genitals as the 'vagina'. This is incorrect—as you would have found out from reading the girls' section, the vagina is only one part. Because a woman's genitals are hidden away, you might need to do a little exploring. If your partner is okay with you looking at her vagina, check it out—spread the lips back and locate her clitoris, it's the little button at the top (it may have a hood over it).

The clitoris is a very important part of the female body: it's the only part of the body, male or female, that is just there for pleasure—everything else has some other use. Did you know that the clitoris is much bigger than the little button that's visible. It goes back into the girl's body then splits into two 'legs'.

Another reason it's important is that most girls require clitoral stimulation to orgasm—imagine if your partner wanted to be sexual with you and they didn't know that your penis was a key to your sexual pleasure!

When I first started my job, a good (female) friend grabbed me by the collar and made sure that I got the message: 'Tell every guy you meet NEVER TOUCH A CLITORIS WITH A DRY FINGER.' So make sure you use some spit, vaginal lubrication or water-based lube.

What's the deal with fanny farts?

When a girl gets turned on, her vagina changes shape—it expands like a balloon, ready to accept a penis. When it expands, it can act like a vacuum and draw air into it. When it shrinks back to normal size, the air can be pushed back out and may make a sound a bit like a fart. This can be embarrassing for her and confusing for you. If you want your partner to feel safe and okay about her body, you'll be cool about it—maybe give her a kiss instead of going, 'Wow! What was that?'

THE G-SPOT

The G-spot is a small cluster of nerve endings that is very sensitive to touch and, when stimulated gently, can provide a girl with great pleasure. The G-spot can be found just inside the vagina, on the front wall. Imagine if you were facing your partner and put your finger into her vagina—if you were to make a 'come here' motion you would be close by. Another approach is to insert two fingers and 'walk' up and down the front wall of her vagina. You might want to ask your partner to guide you by telling you what feels right—for some girls, the area may be oversensitive.

There's also another lesser known cluster of nerve endings called the 'A-spot'. It's further up the front wall of the vagina toward the cervix. And this is why penis size really isn't important. Most of these pleasure centres are located near the entrance of the girl's vagina—the clitoris and G-spot are all within easy reach of most penises.

The G-spot is named after Dr Ernst Gräfenberg and the A-spot, or Anterior Fornix Erogenous Zone, is named after its location on the anterior (toward the front) wall of the vagina.

ORAL SEX

If you're committed to your partner's pleasure, oral sex is worth trying. Some other words people use for oral sex are head, head jobs, face fucking, growling, licking, cunnilingus (licking a girl), going down, rug munching, fellatio (sucking a guy), blow job or eating out. Oral sex is, in a nutshell, when the genitals of one person are stimulated by the mouth of another. And there are techniques to this.

There's a few different methods you may want to try with a female partner:

» Try spelling out the alphabet in cursive with your tongue on and around her clitoris.
» Or try figure 8s.
» Some girls prefer circles.
» Some prefer suction—suck on the clitoris while you stroke it with your tongue.
» Try stroking the clitoris with the underside of your tongue.

Every now and again, move away from the clitoris—maybe pay some attention to her labia or vulva or inner thighs—then come back to the clitoris. As you're licking her, don't forget about the rest of her. Massage her belly, hold hands, look into her eyes—guys can sometimes get a bit too focused on what we're doing. You might want to start masturbating her at the same time. Sometimes this might feel good but it can also be confusing for her. What does she like?

There's a difference between the feelings she gets from her clitoris and the feelings she gets from her G-spot and A-spot (the spots inside a girl's vagina described above). They are extra sensitive because of the high number of nerve endings gathered there. Stimulation of these spots might distract her from the clitoral stimulation. Stimulation to these spots might also make her feel like she needs to pee, but once she moves past that feeling, it can be very enjoyable—or so I've been told.

For guys, it might be a good idea to think about what you like and see if that works for your partner:

» Ask your partner to hold the base of your penis as this can feel great—it's also a good way for them to control your thrusting. You might want to masturbate the shaft while they suck or lick the head of your penis.
» Don't forget about the rest of your body.
» Give feedback—that way you get what feels good—and tell them that the head of your penis is usually a lot more sensitive than the shaft, and the scrotum can be really sensitive too. They might not know this.

Here are even more good tips:

» Get comfortable—be prepared to be there for a while.
» Look for signs your partner is enjoying themself. If you can get eye contact, that's great, or you can pick up their body language. If they're pushing onto you, that's a good sign. If they're pulling away, you might want to try something different—maybe just ask what they'd like you to do.
» Lots of people are concerned about the appearance or the smell of their genitals, and they might not want you to look at them closely. Never push the issue, but some positive feedback might help them feel safer.
» Now is probably not the time to bring it up, but you might want to talk about this later—the type of food they eat, their hygiene and the underwear they use can all affect their smell. Where a girl is in her menstrual cycle can also effect her smell and taste.
» You can make oral sex safer by using a condom or a dam. A dam is a latex sheet that prevents STIs from being transferred during oral sex. It acts as a barrier when placed over a vagina or anus.

Oral sex tip

If you want to receive oral sex, never force your partner's head down onto your penis—it can be a major turn-off and probably a good way to make sure they never give you head again.

If you're going to cum, work out where it's going to go. If you're going to cum in your partner's mouth, let them know so they can make a choice about whether they spit or swallow—it's just good manners.

'DO I UNDERSTAND WHAT MY PARTNER LIKES?'

PENETRATIVE SEX

Whether it's anal or vaginal sex, when it comes to penetration, it's all about angles and access. Some positions provide for deeper penetration—some people like this for the 'filled up' feeling it gives them. Some positions provide greater intimacy—whether it's eye contact or skin-to-skin contact. Some positions allow for greater control, whether it's angle or speed. Some positions provide greater access to the clitoris, and G-, A- or P-spots (prostate).

What's the P-spot?

Anal sex can be even more pleasurable for guys because of the prostate, also known as the P-spot or the 'male G-spot'. The prostate is a small gland in a man's body that is jam-packed with nerve endings so it's very sensitive to the touch.

The P-spot can be accessed through the rectum via the anus. The method for accessing the prostate is very similar to accessing the G-spot in girls. If your partner is in front of you, they insert a well-lubricated finger into the anus and make a come here motion. Find it yourself and then you can give guidance.

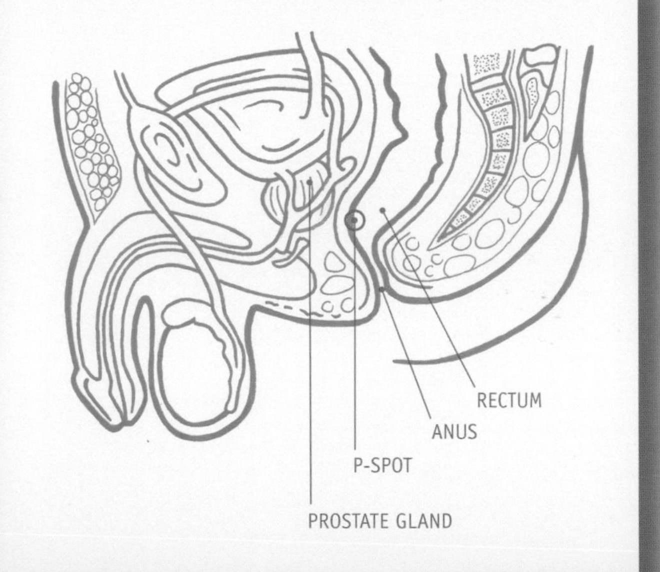

Here's a quick run-down of some positions and what they're good for:

- Accessing the G-spot—girl on top (she can control the angle and depth of penetration); or you standing behind her.
- Accessing the A-spot—deep penetration positions, such as girl on all fours and you kneeling behind her; or girl sitting on the edge of the bed with you kneeling in front of her.
- Clitoral stimulation—missionary position but riding high (put a pillow underneath her bum); or lie on your side with her in front of you (spooning) and stimulate with your hand; or girl on top, facing you and leaning back.
- Accessing the P-spot—missionary position but riding high.

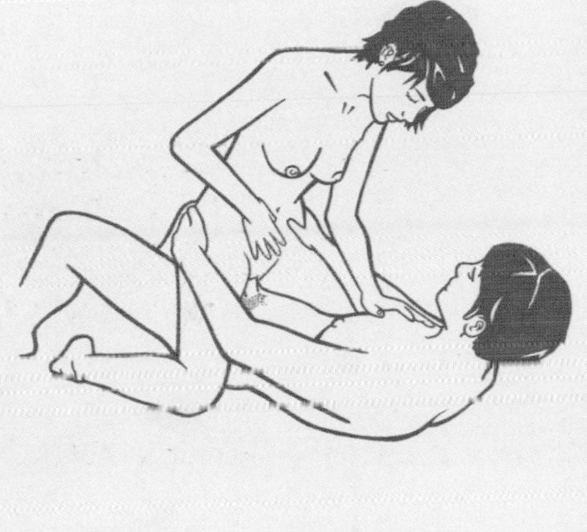

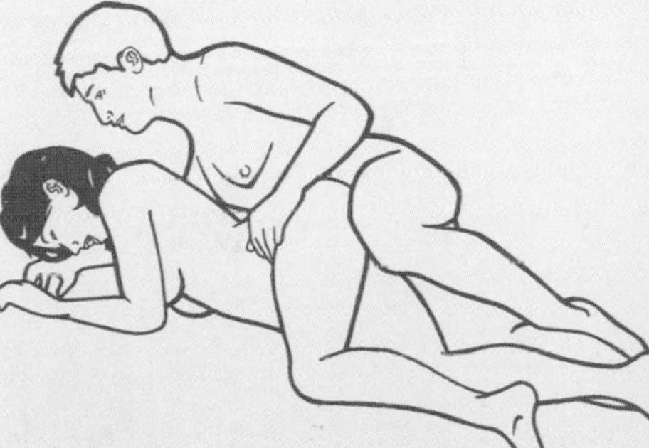

Penetrative sex tip

Sometimes we can get caught up on having to provide our partner with an orgasm. We might try everything but sometimes it just isn't going to happen—there's no point hammering away, you could both end up red raw. Sometimes you just have to let it go and enjoy being with each other without the pressure of 'orgasm'.

ANAL SEX

Whether it's with a tongue, a finger or a penis, lots of people enjoy having their bums pleasured. There're heaps of nerve endings so a bum can provide much enjoyment.

Sometimes people can react badly when their bums are touched—for some guys, it may be homophobia, guilt over enjoying a taboo, or related to negative sexual experiences. Some people don't accept bums as a sexual organ at all—and that's cool too.

I've spoken with some gay guys who were terrified of having anal sex. They really didn't want to. They were operating under a common myth—that all gay guys have anal sex. The reality is that lots of gay couples never have anal sex.

The bottom line (pun intended) is to ask. Like any sexual activity, consent is essential—don't just stick your bits in.

Good tips for anal sex:

» Use lots of lube and go slow.
» Because there's a lot of bacteria in the rectum, you've got to be careful that you don't spread it to your partner's mouth or vagina. Using a dam, condom or glove can be a good way to prevent infection.
» People have two sphincters—the external sphincter that can be voluntarily relaxed and the internal sphincter that requires lots of stimulation to relax.
» A good tip for any anal play is to have a dark-coloured towel nearby to wipe away any stray bits of poo. Emptying your bowels before anal sex can be another way of minimising mess.

Top tips for doing it

Whether it's the first time or the hundredth, you can always get better at sex! Here are some tips to make sex a lot more pleasurable . . .

IN PRAISE OF LUBE

If you only take away one message from this book, remember—lube, lube, LUBE! I've only had a couple of guys approach me on the street to thank me for info about relationships or keeping themselves safe, but heaps of guys have been happy to shout across shopping malls, 'Cheers for the tip about lube!' It's usually when I'm walking with my mum—how does that happen?

Why lube rules:

» It makes everything slide a lot easier.
» It can prevent a condom from tearing.
» It's great to masturbate with—lube wanks rock!
» It increases sensitivity, making sex much more pleasurable.

Make sure your lube is water based. Oil-based stuff like Vaseline or some massage oils can destroy condoms. Lube comes in different flavours (though some flavourings can cause allergic reactions), and you can also get some that heats up or you can get all-natural lubes. There's even a festival in Adelaide that regularly hosts lube wrestling!

Lots of guys I've talked with say they don't need lube because their female partner gets really wet (has lots of natural vaginal lubrication), but vaginal lubrication is meant for skin-on-skin contact, not skin-on-rubber—so any vaginal lubrication can quickly dry out. And the amount of vaginal lubrication can vary depending on where a girl is in her menstrual cycle as well as how horny she feels. Bums don't produce any natural lube so water-based lube is extra useful when it comes to anal sex.

So you get the idea? Sex is better with lube!

There are many brands of lube. Some of the more popular brands are Wetstuff, Glyde, KY-Jelly, Pjur and Durex.

Handy lube

A little bowl of lube or a pump pack can make for hassle-free access. Sachets can be tricky to open in the heat of the moment, and you may need more than one.

TIMING

We might be so keen to have sex that we ignore our partner's needs. If you're having sex with a girl, timing can be extra important—if it were a race to orgasm, guys would win every time. Generally speaking, girls require a bit more time to reach orgasm.

Take it easy—act like there's all the time in the world.

BE COMFORTABLE IN YOUR SKIN

If you're okay with your body, it can make it easier for your partner to be relaxed about their body—even if you have to fake it. The more you practise being nude, the more relaxed you can be with your body. Try it out at home when no one's around, check yourself out in the mirror, and remember to focus on your good points.

Remember that not everyone's body looks the same. If your body doesn't look like the clones that you see in the media, remember that you're real life. Love your body—it makes it easier for others to love it to. Here are some tips on making sure your body feels sexy:

» Be as healthy as you can be—good food, exercise and plenty of sleep are a great start to overall health, including sexual health.

- Smells are funny things. We all release pheromones, kind of like a sex smell. Our natural body odour can be a real turn-on, but stinky foods and poor hygiene can have us releasing pretty toxic odours, kind of like anti-sex smells.
- Shower regularly. You may want to shower together—this can be a good way to nurture your partner.
- Don't try to make up for poor diet or bad hygiene with a heap of deodorants and perfumes. Remember that 'less is more'—a little deodorant on a clean healthy body is always going to smell better than a lot of deodorant on an unhealthy, unwashed body.
- Lots of people swear by citrus foods and pineapple to make their cum taste sweet. On the flip side, coffee and alcohol can make your cum taste awful—you might want to try a home test to see what works for you.
- Avoid stinky or fart-making foods—onions are a classic, or baked beans. Some people's bodies react really badly with dairy products.
- Knowing how your body processes certain foods is a handy body-awareness tool—you can cause serious stomach aches by holding in enormous farts all night long. But it is a special moment in any relationship when you can fart in front of your partner . . . can you believe you just read that?
- Trim your finger and toe nails—especially your fingernails, as they might end up inside your partner.
- Empty your bowels and bladder—nothing can take your mind off the job like needing to poo or pee.
- Some people love facial hair, some hate it—it's up to you and your partner to work that one out.

CREATING SAFETY

Undoubtedly, the most important ingredient for mind-blowing sex is safety. Safety to fully let go of all the hang-ups or insecurities we may have about our body or sex in general.

Create the kind of relationship you want. Talk with your partner. Honesty creates space—if you're honest with your partner, it makes it easier for them to be honest with you. If you want a relationship where you can talk about your deepest desires and fantasies, you need safety. Building trust means not abusing or taking advantage of stuff that's shared in intimate moments.

Make sure your actions back up your words. There's no point sharing secrets if you then go and share your partner's secrets with all your mates. Even if you're fighting with your partner, abusing trust is still abuse.

Consent is essential to a healthy sex life. If someone feels they have to say yes to sex that they don't want, safety goes out the window and resentment starts to build. I don't know about you, but I only want to have sex with people that want to have sex with me.

SENSE OF HUMOUR

Sometimes sex is just funny. Think of a flaccid penis—come on guys lighten up, is there anything funnier in the world?

Beware the passion killers—pressure, stress, guilt, frustration, anger, jealousy, depression, lack of interest, insecurity, lack of respect, worry, sadness, poor self-esteem, shame, fear, negative body image. Humour can relax us—laughing has been shown to have a positive effect on our health. If we can laugh at ourselves, we're much less likely to get stressed. And, if we're not stressed, we are much more likely to have great sex.

FANTASY

Sometimes we get turned on by things we'd like to do, and sometimes by things we'd never want to do—that's the beauty of fantasy. Before you talk about your fantasies, think about it first.

Is your partner likely to be hurt or trust you less because of the fantasy? If so, you've got to ask yourself what's more important to you—the fantasy or your relationship? Is there any chance that the fantasy is degrading—to you or someone else? If so, keep it as fantasy. If you and your partner decide to turn fantasy into reality, make sure you talk about all of the possible outcomes. One way of doing this is to use the POOCH model—What's the **P**roblem? What're your **O**ptions? What are the likely **O**utcomes for each Option ? **C**hoose an option and go with it. **H**ow did it go? Evaluate that option. Would you do it again or are there other options you might want to try?

POST-ORGASM AFFECTION

Sex doesn't have to end after you cum—stroking, cuddling, kissing and licking after ejaculation can be really hot. It's also a good way of showing your partner that they're important to you—not just a sexual object. Remember, there's a person attached to those genitals.

BE PREPARED

Spontaneous, out-of-the-blue sex can be good, but sometimes you might want to set the scene:

» It's all about the flow. First, create a safe space—make sure it is private, minimise interruptions, turn off your phones.
» Next comes ambience. Delight all your senses—soft lighting, fragrant candles, incense or essential oils, nice food like chocolates and fruit to feed each other (and keep your energy up), comfortable space, pillows, nice clean sheets (maybe silky). Make sure it's not too hot or cold.
» If you want, arrange some cool tunes—on repeat.
» And make sure you have plenty of time.

Don't forget that nature can provide lots of sexy, sensory input—crashing thunder, howling wind, soft bird chatter, a warm breeze . . .

COMMUNICATION

For great sex, communication is essential. If you don't like what's going on, talk about it, provide feedback. But remember that communication isn't all verbal—watch your partner's body. How do they respond to your touch? If they're relaxed, it's a good sign that they're enjoying your touch. If they seem tense, maybe chill out for a bit and see what's going on for them.

And watch your own negative thoughts. Sometimes, if our partner says they don't want to be sexual, we hear that they don't want to be with us—two very different things. If you're feeling horny and your partner isn't, maybe take matters into your own hands and masturbate. Or refocus your horniness into intimacy—a cuddle that's just a cuddle. If it's an ongoing issue, talk with your partner about it.

PERIODS 'N' STUFF

Usually when I talk about periods and cycles, guys lean back and go 'Why do we have to hear this stuff?' But by the end of the session, they're leaning forward wanting to know more. Generally, guys don't get to hear this information. I remember when the girls were given the 'talk' at school, we were herded outside to play football. This has kept us in the dark when it comes to things like spot bleeding (bleeding in between periods), PMS (pre-menstrual stress) and ovulation horniness—yes, I said horniness; lots of girls get really horny when they ovulate (release an egg) which happens about halfway through their menstrual cycle.

As for bleeding, lots of guys have spoken with me about finding blood on the sheets or on themselves—they were a bit freaked out, worried that maybe they'd hurt their partner, or that she'd miscarried. While it might be worth getting it checked out, it doesn't necessarily mean something's wrong.

There are lots of myths about PMS—the most damaging one is that it's all in the head. Imagine you're feeling sick and tired, you have a killer headache and pain in your guts, your body feels out of control (just like last month and the month before that), and you're just waiting to bleed . . . then someone says, 'Get over it, it's all in your head'—how would you respond?

The majority of girls suffer with PMS but a minority get support for it. If you want to be a caring partner (or son, brother, or friend), jump onto www.shinesa.org.au and check out the pamphlet about pre-menstrual stress. And flip your book for an in-depth breakdown of what's going on in a menstrual cycle.

'HOW SAFE DO I FEEL ABOUT SEX?'

Accessories—sex toys and fetishes

Lots of people use sex toys to add to their pleasure. Vibrators, dildos, massagers, butterflies, anal beads, cock rings, piercings—the list goes on and on. Some guys fear that they'll be replaced by a vibrator—it never complains and always makes sure the girl orgasms—but I reckon sex toys can be our allies in providing pleasure to our partner. And they can be quite pleasurable to us too—whether we use them internally or against our penis or testicles.

If you're going to share sex toys that you'll insert into each other, condoms are a good way to reduce the risk of infection. And make sure you clean the toys after use.

People can have fetishes for almost anything. The difference between a fetish, as in a sexual accessory, and a hardcore fetish is that with a hardcore fetish someone can't get turned on without a particular object. This can become problematic, but only if the person sees it as a problem. If it's okay with everyone involved then it's okay.

TRICKY QUESTIONS

Q **Why do people sigh, scream and moan during sex?**

A Simple answer: for lots of reasons. It could be pent-up energy building and building and then finding its way out via a groan or a moan. It could be a big sigh after remembering to breathe, or just because sex feels so awesome. Focused breathing transports energy around the body. Moans and groans communicate our desires—and it can be because sex feels really good or really bad, it could be working through some pain or soaking in some pleasure . . . most of all because sounds can be sexy.

Q **Is it cool to use a dildo at my age (15)—I'm a boy, I like it, but is it safe?**

A Dildo's are perfectly safe. If you're inserting them into your anus, remember to use lots of water-based lube and take it easy—relax both your sphincter muscles with some massage and go as slow as you need to. If you're sharing your dildo, a condom can provide some protection from STIs.

Q **How can you tell if your partner is faking an orgasm?**

A The quick answer is you can't—people respond to orgasm in many different ways. You just have to trust that your partner is going to be responsible for their own orgasm, and you can support them by letting them know that their pleasure is important to you and that you're open to feedback. Don't waste headspace on worrying about faking—use it to learn more about your partner's likes and dislikes, be open to simply enjoy what you're doing.

The pressure to orgasm each and every time you have sex can actually get in the way of pleasure. Don't become a 'Did you orgasm that time?' monitor.

Forget about orgasm and enjoy the sensation of being with your partner.

Q **How can I tell my partner that I don't like their sex technique?**

A First off, be really clear about what it is you don't like and why. Is it something that can be improved with a little direction or is it something you're just not into at all?

Sexual incompatibility can be a serious issue in a relationship.

You might want to start by talking about what it is you do like and ask them to focus on that rather than talk about what you don't like. Remember that people are very vulnerable when they're in relationships—and sex can leave us at our most vulnerable, so feedback about our technique, no matter how constructive, may be hurtful. Talking about your wants, needs and desires outside of the bedroom can be useful. It's a brave thing to be honest about getting our needs met, but it's well worth it.

Chapter 6

Safer Sex

'It's good to get comfortable with talking about protection—safety for you and your partner, care and respect—sounds kinda weird but it's like a buffer of comfortness.'

'Wrap it up.'

'It's fun exploring all the things you can do and still stay safe from diseases and pregnancy.'

Safer sex is sex that prevents unplanned pregnancies or STIs and keeps everyone involved free from fear, shame, guilt, exploitation and abuse. Some people prefer to talk about 'safer' sex instead of 'safe' sex, because you can't be 100 per cent safe—there are risks with any sexual behaviour. But, no matter what you call it, it comes down to the same thing—taking care of yourself and your partner.

What gets in the way of safer sex?

The long-term effects of unsafe sex can be pretty huge considering you only need to make one mistake. Some STIs can lead to a reduced quality of life. You might have to manage a chronic condition, and that could mean a heap of pills every day for the rest of your life. Your life may be shortened, you may become infertile (unable to make babies) or, at the other end of the spectrum, you may become a father—another life-long condition!

So why do people still take the chance? Here're some of the reasons given by young people I've talked with:

- lack of information
- lack of condoms/contraception
- drugs and alcohol
- pressure
- 'It will never happen to me' attitude
- not caring
- not thinking past that moment—not worried about the long term
- feeling down, depression—not caring about yourself
- gets in the way of intimacy—one guy said, 'As soon as you cum, you've got to pull out so the sperm don't escape from the condom when your penis goes soft. I like to cuddle and go soft in my girlfriend. Sometimes it makes me feel like my sperm is poison!'

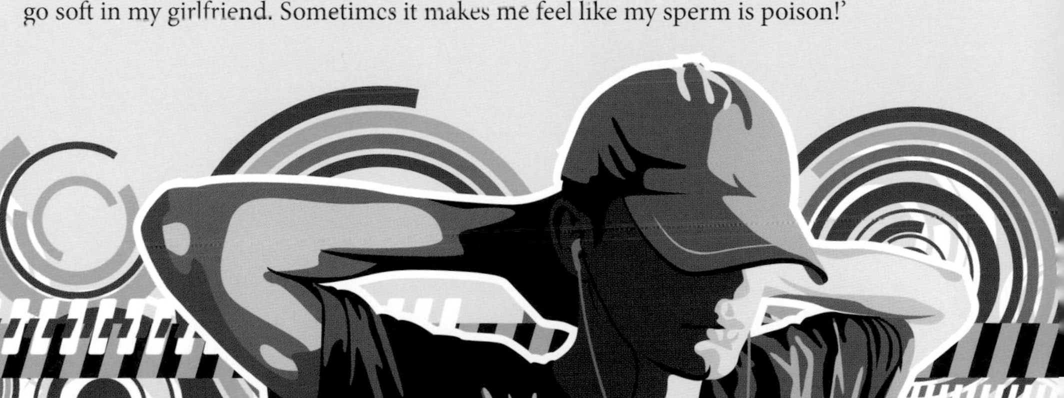

AND THEN THERE'S THE 'CONDOM COMPLAINTS'

Here are some of the reasons people give for not using condoms . . . and some of my responses:

- There wasn't any available: I encourage guys to have stashes of condoms everywhere—in their room, at their mates' houses, at their partner's house. You can get condoms just about anywhere; some organisations will even mail them to you, so lack of availability shouldn't be an issue.
- Condoms mean there's a lack of trust: Using condoms means you respect yourselves and each other enough to look after your health.
- I lose my hard-on when I see a condom: Sometimes guys can lose their erections while putting on a condom; it might break the mood or they might start thinking of pregnancy or diseases. Try and turn it into a sex toy while you're on your own, so there's no pressure from your partner. Try masturbating with a condom—don't forget the lube. Train your mind so that when you see a condom, you think SEX, not disease or pregnancy. The more you practise the easier it gets.
- Condoms get in the way or break the mood: Not as much as small children! Try feeling sexy after changing pooey nappies all day. Seriously, though, make condoms part of your sex play. Maybe have a nice lube wank while putting it on, or your partner might want to try putting it on, maybe with their mouth—but watch out for teeth! Another tip is to get condoms ready before you get too heavy. Always have them close to your bed. If you're pretty sure you're going to have sex, open one or two so they're ready to go when you are. This way, you keep the flow going.
- I can't get any big enough/I can't get any small enough: Just like penises, condoms come in lots of shapes, sizes and colours. Look around until you find the one that suits you best. You can also get thicker condoms for anal sex. And as for the too big stuff, people blow condoms up and put them on their heads—if your penis is as big as someone's head, I'm sure a company will sponsor you and make up a special batch just for you.
- Condoms always break: The modern condom is a pretty effective piece of equipment. If they break, it's usually because they weren't used correctly. Maybe they were out of date or not stored correctly or there wasn't any lube.
- I'm allergic to latex: You can get polyurethane condoms.
- Condoms reduce sensitivity—'It's like wearing a raincoat in the shower': Some guys like the reduced sensitivity as it means they can last longer. But in the interests of pleasure, I recommend a couple of drops of lube (only a couple of drops, otherwise you risk the condom coming off) on the head of your penis before you roll the condom on as this can greatly increase the pleasure of the wearer.

1 OPEN THE PACKET CAREFULLY

2 SQUEEZE THE AIR OUT OF THE TIP OF THE CONDOM

3 UNROLL THE CONDOM TO THE BASE OF THE STIFF PENIS

4 APPLY LOTS OF WATER-BASED LUBRICANT TO THE OUTSIDE OF THE CONDOM

5 AFTER CUMMING HOLD THE CONDOM AT THE BASE WHEN PULLING OUT

6 DISPOSE OF CONDOM CAREFULLY

'IS IT WORTH IT IF I DON'T USE A CONDOM? WHAT DO I THINK WILL HAPPEN?'

Why condoms rule

They're cheap (and often free at youth or health centres).

They're the only contraceptive method that can protect you against STIs—but remember, condoms only protect the parts they're covering, they don't protect against STIs around the genital area.

They're the only contraceptive method that guys have any control over—except for getting a vasectomy (getting your vas deferens cut) and that's usually for older guys who have already had kids.

You can get them just about everywhere (if you can't get them near you, contact your nearest youth, health or community centre and get them to do something about it).

TIPS FOR USING CONDOMS

- Always have a few just in case one breaks. You may even want to have sex more than once. It's always good to have a stash so you can practise putting them on—it's like any skill, the more you practise the better you get at it.
- What if I roll it on the wrong way? Throw it away—if you turn it over, you could pass on an STI or get someone pregnant with the pre-cum that may have been on the tip of your penis (pre-cum is a mix of urine, sperm and semen—it comes out of the tip of the penis when it gets erect and is basically the urethra (see diagram on page 22) cleaning itself in readiness for the next batch of cum).
- Store your condoms properly. Keep them in a cool place, out of direct sunlight—maybe in your bedside drawer, or even in the fridge. I've heard of parents who keep a well-stocked supply in the fruit bowl so anyone can grab some without embarrassment (note to parents: make sure you supply lube too).
- It's okay to leave them in the car for the night but take them out when you get home. If they've been exposed to heat, throw them away—it's not worth taking the chance.
- Some people are allergic to latex and they might not even know it—until they start getting a reaction from using condoms. If you have latex allergies, use polyurethane condoms—and it's all good.
- Am I safer if I use two condoms at once? No—they can catch on each other and tear or you may lose one inside your partner!
- Don't flush 'em—they have a nasty habit of floating back up and they're not environmentally friendly.
- Perhaps, most importantly, if you use condoms, do so willingly. Don't keep complaining about having to use them—that's emotional blackmail.

WHAT IF THE CONDOM BREAKS DURING SEX?

STOP! You can continue being sexual if you want to, but in some other way that won't increase your chances of infection or pregnancy. If you continue having penis-in-vagina sex, you might push some pre-cum (containing virus, bacteria or active sperm) up through the cervix into the uterus, where it is a lot more sperm friendly.

It might be a good idea to get an STI test. If you were having sex with a female and she wasn't using any other contraception, she can use emergency contraception (EC) to prevent pregnancy (see 'Contraception', later in this chapter, for more details).

If there's a chance you or your partner has HIV, you can contact your state AIDS Council for information on post-exposure prophylaxis (PEP). This is a course of drugs that may prevent the virus from taking off, but it's most effective within 72 hours from possible infection so don't wait around thinking about it.

IS THERE SEX WITHOUT CONDOMS?

What if you and your partner absolutely, positively, 100 per cent don't want to use condoms—are there any options? Well, there aren't many, but here's a few:

- One option is to not have any kind of sex—that's 100 per cent safe.
- Oral sex is a little safer than penetrative sex—you can't get pregnant but you can still catch STIs.
- Masturbation is also safer than penetrative sex—but you can still pass on STIs via your hands.
- Another option is for you and your partner to get tested for STIs (a good idea anyway) to make sure that you won't give each other anything, then use some other form of contraception (not necessary if your partner's a guy). As long as that contraceptive method is reliable and neither of you have sex with anyone else, you may be protected. Honesty, trust and commitment play a big part in keeping you and your partner safe.

Conception and contraception—what guys need to know

This section is about contraception in relation to guys—if you want more information on contraception, flip your book and check out the details on contraception in the girls' section, or go to www.shinesa.org.au.

So with conception (making a baby) the idea is to get a sperm and an egg together. With contraception (preventing a pregnancy) the idea is to keep them apart either with a barrier method (like a condom) or a hormonal method. Some hormones can trick the body into stopping the release of the egg from the ovaries, making the lining of the uterus un-eggfriendly. Others can make the mucus at the cervix thicker to prevent any sperm from entering the uterus and making its way to the fallopian tubes and any potential eggs that might be waiting around.

Using a barrier method as well as a hormonal method is a great way to double your protection from unplanned pregnancy.

As I've said, condoms are the only contraceptive method a guy can control, but we can take responsibility in other ways. For a start we can find out how contraception works, which ones our partner uses and what support they'd like from us. Maybe a reminder to take the pill, or perhaps we could share the cost or even pay for it all—after all, she's taking the health risks and side-effects.

Show your support by going along with your partner to doctor's appointments—ask questions, be interested. If your partner doesn't want to use another method of contraception other than condoms, it's really important that you support her decision. There can be lots of side-effects

from using hormonal contraception—would you be willing to put up with headaches, nausea, sore breasts, acne or mood swings?

THE CONTRACEPTIVE PILL

If your girlfriend is on the contraceptive pill, keep a spare packet at your place just in case she forgets or runs out while she's there. But make sure it's her prescription—not all pills are the same.

A girl has to take the contraceptive pill at roughly the same time every day. If she doesn't take them at the set time or forgets one, you may have to use condoms or not have sex until she has contraceptive cover again. Flip your book for more information on the timing of the contraceptive pill.

THE WITHDRAWAL METHOD

Many guys say to their girlfriend, 'I'll pull out before I cum?' The withdrawal method is unsafe for a few reasons: there may be pre-cum on the tip of your penis, or control might go out the window at the crucial time (as in 'I'm going to pull out, I'm going to pull out . . . oops too late').

EMERGENCY CONTRACEPTION

Emergency contraception (EC) is a high dose contraceptive pill. It's not recommended for regular use. The emergency pill is effective up to five days after unprotected sex, but the sooner it's used, the more effective it is.

You can get it from doctors, sexual health clinics, emergency departments in hospitals and most chemists.

IS SEX WHEN SHE HAS HER PERIOD A FORM OF CONTRACEPTION?

No! A woman is generally only fertile for one day out of 28 (roughly) and that day is usually in between her periods—but a woman can release an egg at any time without knowing it. Also, sperm can last up to a week inside a girl's uterus and fallopian tubes. So even if you have sex during her period, she can still get pregnant.

'IS MY GIRLFRIEND TAKING CONTRACEPTION AND HOW CAN I SUPPORT HER?'

Sexually transmissible infections (STIs)

STIs are also called STDs (sexually transmitted diseases)—so what's the difference? Nothing. They're the same thing. It doesn't really matter what you call them, it only matters that you know about them.

STIs are spread by skin-to-skin contact or sharing body fluids (blood, semen, vaginal discharge or anal mucus) or they can crawl (pubic lice or scabies). Not all STIs are sexually transmitted. Scabies and pubic lice (crabs) can be spread from sharing a bed, towels or clothes. Even though it's not technically an STI, hepatitis C can be spread by sharing toothbrushes or razors, and both hepatitis C and HIV can be spread by sharing needles.

For a list of the common STIs, what they are and how they're transmitted, check out the information in the girls' section. As guys we've got our very own STI. It's called non-specific urethritis or NSU; this causes a burning sensation when you urinate and can have an unusual discharge (mucus) from your penis—luckily it's easily treated with antibiotics.

STI SYMPTOMS

So what are we looking for? Unusual lumps, bumps, rashes, pimples, pain when urinating, flu-like symptoms, generally feeling unwell, blisters, unusual smell, unusual discharge (not urine, semen or smegma), or patchy loss of hair. You might get itchy or you may actually see pubic lice.

Most importantly—**there may be no symptoms at all.**

Many of the STI symptoms listed above could be due to other conditions so there's only one way to find out—get tested.

TESTING FOR STIs

You can't tell who's got an STI by the way they look, dress or act—even if you have a good look over all of their bits. Some STIs have no symptoms at all so you may not know that you've got one. The only way to be sure is to get tested.

STIs can cause tension in a relationship if one or both of you have a flare-up. For example, if one of you has herpes but hasn't had a flare-up for years, you might think that you're cured but the virus is still in your body. Viruses thrive on stress, so imagine you're three months into the relationship, maybe the honeymoon period is over, you're starting to worry about the relationship and bang—a big blister appears on you or your partner's genitals. You might blame each other for passing it on, or think that your partner has been unfaithful.

I reckon it's worth getting tested before becoming sexually active in a new relationship—at least then you know what you're dealing with.

You can get tested at your doctor's, at some hospitals or at some health or youth centres. There may even be a specialised STI clinic near you. Along with the physical symptoms, as a result of an STI you may feel angry, shamed, betrayed, sad, scared or all of the above. A good clinician will

talk about this stuff when you're getting tested. They will also talk to you about things like getting your results and treatment—if they don't, find one who will.

TREATMENT

Time for the good news: most STIs can be cured with antibiotics or lotions and potions; the body can even cure some on its own. However, some STIs stay in your body forever and require you to look after your health—viruses love stress and sickness. Some of these require ongoing medication.

The most important thing is to make yourself aware—by getting tested. Then you'll know if it's an STI that can be cured, or if it's one that can be managed.

STIs AND TREATMENT CHART

BACTERIA
Curable with antibiotics

- SYPHILIS
- GONORRHOEA
- CHLAMYDIA
- NON-SPECIFIC URETHRITIS
- GARDNERELLA
- PELVIC INFLAMMATORY DISEASE
- TRICHOMONIASIS

VIRUS
Symptoms treated and the virus leaves the body, some viruses stay in the body and symptoms can return

- GENITAL HERPES — Remains in the body with return episodes
- GENITAL WARTS — Remains in the body or may reappear
- WART VIRUS — Remains in the body or may reappear
- HEPATITIS A — Remains in the body or can leave the body
- HEPATITIS B — Remains in the body or can leave the body
- HEPATITIS C — Remains in the body or can leave the body
- HIV/AIDS

FUNGUS
Curable with anti-fungal cream

- THRUSH (Candida)

MITES
Curable with body paints and special shampoo

- SCABIES
- PUBIC LICE (Crabs)

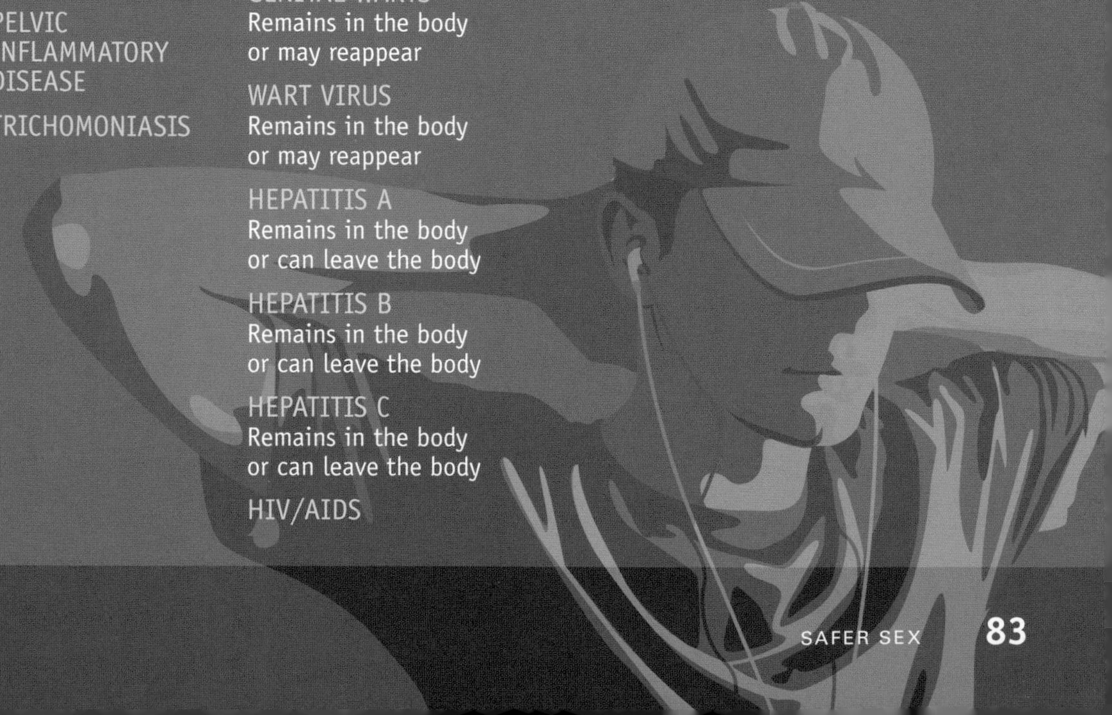

PREVENTION

Remember, condoms and water-based lube are the best protection against STIs. Dams are a great form of protection for oral sex. Condoms are a way of protecting your penis during oral sex too.

Try not to brush your teeth or eat sharp foods like corn chips just before having oral sex. These can make little cuts in your mouth that may allow STIs into your blood stream.

If you have open sores or blisters, try and keep them away from your partner if possible. Look out for nicks, scratches and cuts on your hands. These are all ways that STIs can be transmitted. One way to protect your hands is with latex gloves—they may not be very romantic but like condoms, you could turn it into part of your sex play.

Be careful with your piercings—they can tear condoms. Also, tongues never heal while a piercing is still in, so they can be an entry point for STIs.

Talking about STIs with a partner is really important. A big part of sexual ethics is honesty. If you may be exposing your partner to any harm, it's best to make them fully aware of the risks they're taking. It might be a hard conversation, but it can be a harder conversation later on if you pass on an infection.

There are many conditions that can cause a lot of worry but aren't necessarily dangerous. Skin tags may look like warts, cysts in your scrotum might feel like cancer, pearly penile papules or skin rashes on your penis might look like symptoms of an STI but they're all harmless. However, you must get any changes checked out so you know what you're dealing with.

KEEP IT CLEAN . . . AND DRY

Wash regularly. If you're uncircumcised, smegma (cheesy stuff) can build up under the foreskin. Don't worry, it's a natural by-product made up of oils from the skin, old skin cells and bacteria, but if it's not washed away regularly, it will build up and the bacteria will get out of control and stink. So wash under your foreskin daily with water and mild soap. And make sure you dry yourself properly as moist conditions can lead to a condition called balanitis.

TRICKY QUESTIONS

Q **What's the difference between HIV and AIDS?**

A HIV (human immuno-deficiency virus) is the actual virus that causes the immune system to break down and this lets other infections into the body. When someone has one or more of these opportunistic infections they're said to have acquired immune deficiency syndrome (AIDS).

Q **Can pre-cum get a girl pregnant?**

A When a penis gets erect it cleans itself—squeezing out any old cum or urine that might be sitting in the urethra. This makes it nice and clean for the next ejaculation. This fluid is called pre-cum and as it may contain sperm there is a possibility that it can make a girl pregnant. Pre-cum can also contain virus and bacteria, so it's possible to pass on an STI as well.

Q **What's the most common STI in Australia?**

A The most common STI is also one of the easiest to treat. Chlamydia is a bacterial infection that can be cured with antibiotics. One of the reasons chlamydia is so prevalent is that it can have no symptoms so someone with chlamydia might not even know it and unknowingly spread it around.

Q **How can you tell if someone has an STI?**

A You often can't. STIs don't discriminate—all kinds of people get STIs. A visit to your local clinic should confirm that: there'll be sports folks, business people, arty folks, young people, older people, men, women—everyone. Many infections don't always have visible symptoms so you can inspect someone from head to toe with a bright light and still not find anything, but that doesn't mean they haven't got anything. The only way to know what you're dealing with is to get tested.

Q **My partner was diagnosed with chlamydia. What should I do?**

A Get tested too. It's important that you get tested and receive treatment if required to avoid re-infecting your partner.

Chapter 7

When Things Get Tricky

'Sex isn't easy; it's good to know that you're not the only one to have dramas. Had I known that, I'd have felt a lot better about it.'

'Denial is tempting but it sucks. Trying to forget about it, hoping it will just go away gets you nowhere. Communication is the best option.'

'I tried to talk to people, but I don't think anyone wanted to hear.'

Sexual violence, childhood sexual abuse, sexual difficulties—there's a bunch of reasons why there's silence about these issues, but more reasons why we should be shouting from the rooftops.

Sometimes just talking about our need for intimacy can be hard for guys. It can be seen as unmanly for guys to talk about fear or confusion about sex. It's about time we stopped shutting ourselves and our mates down—how can you make space for these conversations?

Sexual violence

Sexual violence includes things like childhood sexual abuse (an adult involving a child in *any* sexual behaviour) or sexual assault. Sexual violence can affect everyone—it could be a friend or family member, it could be your partner, it might even be you. Research suggests that one in three young women and one in five young men have experienced unwanted sexual contact before they turn 18 years of age. Young people and people with disabilities and mental health problems have an increased risk of sexual assault.

It makes me sad to say it, but the majority of violence in relationships is perpetrated by guys. It doesn't matter where you come from, how much money you have, whether you're gay or heterosexual, abuse is not acceptable.

Most people think of violence as physical stuff, like hitting, but it comes in many forms. It could be telling someone what to wear, who they can mix with, what they can do, what they spend their money on, or what you do together sexually. It can be generally making them feel bad or unsafe through humiliation, threats or put-downs. It's never okay for anyone, guys or girls, to act in these ways.

If you find yourself acting in controlling or abusive ways, it really is time to put a stop to it. You may have learned that that's what it means to be a man, if that's how all the men in your life act. Maybe that's how you've been treated by the people that are meant to love you. *It doesn't have to be that way.*

Stopping the cycle of violence (people treating you badly so you pass it on) is taking responsibility for your own shit—taking out your anger on other people is never okay. As guys we have a role to challenge this stuff. Let's not pass it on to the next generation. For more information, go to www.endabuse.org.

Alcohol and other drugs

Alcohol and drugs can lead to abusive behaviour, and can definitely get in the way of healthy relationships and great sex—especially in the long term. On the other hand, many people choose to use alcohol and drugs and still have healthy relationships.

'AM I VIOLENT, CONTROLLING OR ABUSIVE?'

Drugs and alcohol may make us feel more relaxed and break down our inhibitions, but they can also affect the decisions we make. It's a good idea to be 100 per cent clear with yourself—while you're sober/straight—about what you're willing to do and what risks you are taking . . . And you might want to have some condoms and lube 'just in case'.

Problem drug use raises some big questions (not to be answered when high). I always ask guys what means more to them—getting high or being in their relationship? I also ask their partners if they're prepared to be in a relationship with someone who's going to continue to use drugs. They're tough questions—especially if you're in love. It's never a good idea to go into a relationship thinking you're going to change someone, but it can get a bit boring being in a relationship with someone who's always off their face. Alcohol or drug use is never an excuse for violence or abuse.

'IS MY DRUG USE GETTING IN THE WAY OF MY RELATIONSHIPS?'

Sexual assault

The term 'sexual assault' covers:

- sexual harassment—unwanted sexualised questions, dirty jokes, repeated pick-up lines
- indecent assault—unwanted masturbation, touching or fondling
- rape—unwanted oral, anal or vaginal penetration by a penis, object or any part of the body
- coercion—sex without consent, a victim is bullied, tricked or threatened.

WHY DON'T PEOPLE REPORT IT?

It's estimated that only 15 per cent of all sexual assaults are reported. So why don't more people file reports?

Fear of further violence, self-blame (the victim may believe that they somehow deserved what they got because of what they were doing or wearing or how they were acting), not recognising it as violence, or fear of not being believed can get in the way of people speaking up.

With guys, there can be extra barriers to reporting. These include:

- homophobia—as most perpetrators are male, victims might fear being labelled as homosexual. It can be extra tricky if the victim got an erection or ejaculated—this doesn't mean he enjoyed it, it could be just a physical response
- the idea that men can't be victims because victims are weak—it would be admitting that someone had power over you
- the perpetrator might have been a woman so to admit that a woman had power over you might be an extra humiliation
- there's a myth that all victims become perpetrators—this can stop guys from talking about their abuse for fear of being labelled as potential offenders.

If you've experienced sexual violence, it can feel like a life sentence. Some people talk about feeling like they're damaged goods or out of control. But it is possible to regain control. It might take time and hard work to heal—support can be useful—but it's possible to move from being a victim to a survivor to a thriver.

SUPPORTING A SURVIVOR OF SEXUAL VIOLENCE

Some reactions are useful, some aren't . . . Listening, believing and supporting are good. Blaming or pressuring the person to get counselling, report to police or forget about it might not be so useful.

A couple of useful books are *The Courage to Heal Workbook for Male and Female Survivors of Childhood Sexual Abuse* by Laura Davis and *It Happened to Me: A teen's guide to overcoming sexual abuse* by William Lee Carter. You can order these online, but lots of libraries or health centres may have a copy you can borrow. Or you could contact one of the agencies or websites listed in the resources section of this book.

TAKING A STAND

It's up to us guys to take a stand against sexual violence. But how?

One thing we can do is raise awareness of the amount and impact of sexual violence. Challenge other guys—it might be over a joke, or one of your mates getting a girl drunk to have sex with her, or putting down someone who's been raped, or watching pornography that has staged or real sexual violence. If you don't challenge, you may give other guys the idea that sexual violence is okay.

In 2001, the Office of Crime Statistics found that 96.5 per cent of alleged offenders for all sexual offences were male. Most perpetrators are men, but remember, most men don't perpetrate.

Mental health, depression, anxiety and sex

Despite the fact that one in five Australians experience a mental illness at some time in their lives, it is still a taboo in our society. The effects on our sexuality can be crippling. Relating to people can be a chore, sexual functioning might be affected by our moods or medication.

If mental illness is affecting your relationships or sex life, bring it up with your doctor—it might be embarrassing but, if they don't know what's going on for you, they can't support you to make changes.

Termination

One of the hardest conversations I have is with guys who don't want their partner to have a termination (abortion). The bottom line is guys often don't have a say in the matter. It's the girl's body that's being put at risk by pregnancy and birth or the termination so it's 100 per cent her choice. All I can suggest is that you support your partner at this very difficult time. Girls don't make these choices lightly and their decision should be respected.

Open communication is vital. Offer your support. She might want you to go with her to the appointment or she might want to go alone or with a friend; but at least if you've offered support, she'll know you care.

Supporting her decision doesn't mean you have to like it—many guys feel angry or sad, powerless or betrayed, and these are all reasonable reactions. If you want support to work out what's going on for you, contact one of the organisations or websites in the resources section.

Sexual difficulties

The 'Australian study of health and relationships' (2002) explored sexual difficulties that participants had experienced for at least one month in the last year. The research found that the following were most common:

» lack of interest in sex (24.9 per cent of men and 54.8 per cent of women)
» coming to orgasm too quickly (23.8 per cent of men and 11.7 per cent of women)
» not having an orgasm (6.3 per cent of men and 28.6 per cent of women)
» not enjoying sex (5.6 per cent of men and 27.3 per cent of women)
» physical pain (2.4 per cent of men and 20.3 per cent of women)
» worry about body image (14.2 per cent of men and 35.9 per cent of women).

Some sexual difficulties can lead to other difficulties. Performance anxiety (being stressed over performing sexually) may cause you to cum too quickly, or have trouble getting a hard-on, which may result in a lack of interest in sex, which can lead to desire discrepancy, which can lead to performance anxiety, and around we go again.

With most sexual difficulties, there can be a combination of causes. Some may be physical—such as infection, injury or pain. Others may be psychological—such as past sexual trauma or abuse, anxiety, inexperience or depression, or there might be a reaction to medication or your environment.

The trick is to match the cure to the cause. And sometimes it can take a bit of unravelling to get to the root cause. A counsellor or therapist can help you identify what's going on.

With all of these situations the support of a partner is useful but not always available. We might be embarrassed to talk about it or we might not have a partner.

If you are experiencing any of these difficulties, or your partner is, please contact one of the agencies or websites in the resources section of this book.

LACK OF INTEREST IN SEX

Not being interested in sex goes against the myth that guys are always ready for sex. There're plenty of reasons why guys might not be interested in sex: they might be tired, sick, stressed or sad. It could be that they're just not interested. Some folks see themselves as asexual. Or there could just be other things going on at the moment. They might be in a relationship that they don't want to be in. Lack of interest in sex is one of those things that people like to turn into an issue—if it's not a problem for you and your partner, then that's cool.

PREMATURE EJACULATION

Most guys have experienced or will experience cumming before they want to. Lots of people ask, 'How soon is too soon?' If you cum after 10 minutes and that's okay with you and your partner, then that's fine. It's only a problem if you cum before you want to. Talk about frustration.

Sulking, ranting and raving, giving yourself a hard time, or blaming your partner is a real turn-off. Remember, sex is more than 'sticking it in'. Just as we've learned to cum quickly, we can re-learn to enjoy the ride by focusing on intimacy and foreplay and making each other feel good.

Fixing the problem takes commitment, but it will be well worth it to have a satisfying sex life. I've included some techniques to overcome premature ejaculation because it's one of the biggest causes of concern for young guys and is often easily treated. Beware of the many quick fix 'cures' out there which don't really fix the problem—at their worst they can make sex less enjoyable, at their best they're a crutch not a cure, and some simply don't work.

Stop/start, or squeeze?

The two main techniques for overcoming premature ejaculation are the 'stop/start' and the 'squeeze' methods as pioneered by researchers William Masters and Virginia Johnson. Both begin by practising with masturbation on your own so you can notice when you're about to cum. When you feel like you're about to cum, stop masturbating (as in the stop/start) or squeeze (as in the squeeze) your penis at the base of the head (remember to be gentle). After the urge to cum goes away, start masturbating again. Each time you practise, try to go longer before you ejaculate.

Once you feel ready, it's time to move up a step. Repeat the process with your partner masturbating you—this relies on good communication skills and having a supportive partner. Let your partner know when you feel like you're about to cum and get them to squeeze or stop. Start again when the urge has gone.

The next step is to practise with your partner masturbating you while you're touching their

body. Move on to being inside your partner without moving, just be inside of them—if you feel you're about to cum, stop or withdraw and squeeze.

When you're ready, start moving but, as soon as you feel like you're going to cum, stop or withdraw and squeeze. It's up to you how quickly you move through these phases. But try and go longer each time until you and your partner are satisfied.

What else can you do?

Another way to deal with premature ejaculation is to cum as usual then be sexual in other ways—remember your whole body is a sexual organ. Then when you're ready, try again.

Exercising your pelvic floor muscles (called Kegel exercises) is an excellent way to get control over your ejaculation. Flex those muscles that help you to stop urinating mid-flow. These exercises may also provide you with more intense orgasms.

Never give up! If these techniques don't work, contact one of the agencies or websites in the 'Learning More' resources section.

NOT HAVING AN ORGASM

The stats suggest it's not a common problem for guys, but it's a huge problem for our girls. Flip your book to see what girls think about orgasm.

Some of the porn-fed myths about orgasm are that sex always ends in orgasm and, more specifically, that sex always ends after the *guy* orgasms. This can encourage us to think that our orgasm is the only goal—we might forget about our partner and our shared pleasure along the way.

Another porn-fed myth is that girls always orgasm during penis-in-vagina sex. The reality is that many girls *don't* orgasm during penis-in-vagina sex, they may require clitoral stimulation and some girls may never have an orgasm.

There can be a number of reasons why people are unable to orgasm. They might not feel comfortable either physically or emotionally, or they might hold onto negative messages about sex, fearing they are doing something bad or dirty.

Your partner's orgasm is their responsibility, but it might be a good idea to ask if there is any way you can support them. It might be using some technique tips or simply letting them know that their pleasure is important to you too—avoid putting more pressure onto either of you; sex is about pleasure not performance.

NOT ENJOYING SEX

Sometimes people have sex they're not enjoying to please their partner—but if most partners knew this, they'd be horrified. There's no rule that says you have to like sex, but having sex that we don't enjoy can have a serious impact on our health and wellbeing. If you want to enjoy sex but don't, contact one of the agencies or websites in the resources section of this book.

PAINFUL SEX

Although not identified as a huge issue for guys, it *is* our issue if we want our girlfriends to enjoy sex. There's a number of reasons for painful sex—there might not be any or enough lubrication, an infection or an allergic reaction to the condom or the lube could cause discomfort, there could be too much friction, or a strain.

The bottom line is—if sex is painful, stop, get checked out to see what's going on. That way you can start to do something about it.

ERECTILE DIFFICULTIES

In younger guys, trouble getting or keeping an erection is usually related to the use of alcohol or other drugs. Did you know that smoking cigarettes affects your blood pressure? Erections rely on blood pressure so the cigarette you have now can prevent you from having erections later on in life—they should put that on cigarette packets!

Some 'cures' can be dangerous—some vacuum pumps can damage the penis and some drugs (including Viagra) can be unsafe in certain conditions.

For more info go to www.andrologyaustralia.org.

DESIRE DISCREPANCY

Our libido (or sex drive) can be affected by many things—stress, illness, menstrual cycles, unresolved conflict in the relationship. It's important to have realistic expectations when it comes to desire. And it's unrealistic to expect that you and your partner will have perfectly matched levels of desire all of the time, if ever.

Desire discrepancy can affect the whole relationship. Open and honest communication is a good start to finding out what's going on; from there you can explore opportunities for treatment—lifestyle changes, relationship changes, and medical treatment and counselling have all proven useful in balancing out expectations and levels of desire.

VAGINISMUS

Vaginismus is a condition where the muscles around the vagina spasm and clamp shut. This can happen for a range of reasons. It might be that the girl is feeling nervous, unsafe or isn't ready for sex, she may have suffered sexual trauma or abuse, or it might be related to an infection or pain. I've spoken with lots of guys who've had trouble 'finding the hole'—it might have been due to vaginismus.

PERFORMANCE ANXIETY

Can I keep it up? Will I go for long enough? Will I satisfy my partner? Am I big enough? Anxiety about our performance can affect our performance—what a vicious circle!

We can get so caught up in our heads that we forget to 'be' in our bodies and enjoy being intimate with someone. If you can, talk with your partner about your fears and questions—chances are, they'll have some of the same things going on for them.

'WHO DO I KNOW THAT I CAN FREELY AND OPENLY TALK TO ABOUT SEX?'

Getting support

When it comes to sexual health, getting support can be really hard. Embarrassment can impact on our health. Getting correct information is important. In the resources section, there's a list of websites that provide factual information—you can contact most of them if you have specific questions. Your local library is another good source of info.

Sometimes you need more than information—you might need counselling or medical treatment, or you might need to talk to someone to get a bit of a reality check.

A phone helpline is a good way to get support without exposing yourself too much. Drawbacks are that people can't run tests and see for themselves what's going on, but a phone conversation might help ease you into the idea of getting support.

Sometimes it can be hard for guys to accept support—some guys see it as weak. But I reckon looking after your health and wellbeing is a strong thing to do, and it's better than struggling on in denial.

SUSSING PEOPLE OUT

Not everyone is okay about discussing sex. They might be embarrassed or believe that it's not something to be talked about. They might react in a range of ways—from useful to scary or damaging. If someone reacts in a negative way, that's their issue—just because they can't handle it doesn't mean you're weird, bad or wrong. There will be other people who will give you the support you need.

So how do you know if someone's going to be good to talk to? Who can you trust? What about the people around you? Parents or carers, friends, family members, teachers, coaches or instructors, religious or spiritual leaders or your doctor? What attitudes do they have about sex and sexuality? Can you talk with them?

See how they respond when you raise sex-related topics. You don't have to start by talking about yourself; try raising issues like sexual education at your school or an article in the newspaper—there're always plenty of opportunities. It can be a good chance to learn together.

Adults usually want to support you, but they might not know how. Some research with parents showed that 99 per cent thought it was important to talk to their children about sexuality and relationships, but 59 per cent said that there was a number of barriers including cultural issues, embarrassment, lack of knowledge and a lack of confidence (*Pathways and Barriers: Parent research project report*, SHine SA, 2004).

If you do find someone who's safe to talk to, tell your friends—it's always handy to know where to get good support.

GOING PRO

If you've decided to go to your doctor or a sexual health clinic—what's next? Some clinics have special drop-in times, but for most you'll have to make an appointment. You might have to pay or you might need to bring along a health care or Medicare card—it's good to check this stuff out when you make an appointment.

Taking along a support person is a good idea. It's best if you can have your parents' or caregivers' support, but it isn't always that easy. Sometimes when we're in a stressful situation, we can forget vital information. Before making an appointment, write down everything that you want to talk about. At the front counter you usually don't have to go into all the details, just the service you require, like a STI test or counselling or information.

Some people prefer to go to a clinic that's far from where they live to avoid the chances of running into someone they know—be prepared, it still might happen. One thing to keep in mind is that you're not doing anything shameful, you're looking after your health. In your first appointment, the doctor or nurse will record your sexual history (what you've been doing sexually). They need to know what kind of sex you've been having so they can do an accurate risk assessment and provide you with the right service. This is where honesty is vital.

TESTING

Most pregnancy tests require the girl to provide a urine sample. If your girlfriend is going for a pregnancy test, she might really appreciate your support—a potential pregnancy can raise many relationship issues.

Most STIs can be detected visually or by a blood or urine test. Drink lots of water and try not to urinate before going to the clinic. Some STIs are notifiable—that means if you test positive for one of these, the clinic will notify the relevant health department. They might give you the opportunity to contact your previous partners or offer to contact them for you. They won't give them your name, but will let them know they may have been exposed to an infection and ask them to arrange a check-up. This is important for preventing further infection.

GETTING YOUR RESULTS

It can be really useful to think ahead about possible results and be aware of your options. How could it impact on your life? What support is available? Your doctor or nurse will talk with you about this stuff—if they don't, ask for more information.

Pregnancy tests can usually provide a result within a few minutes, but STI results can take up to a week. And the window period (the time it takes for an infection to show up in your blood) for HIV can be from three to six months. These can be stressful times in the relationship—a partner's support can really help.

Most services require you to come in for another appointment to receive STI results to ensure confidentiality and provide support.

COUNSELLING

Different counsellors work in different ways, but it's good to have some bottom-line expectations. Expect to be treated with respect, to feel safe, to be believed and listened to. If a counsellor doesn't do this, find someone else. Lots of people who talk about counselling in a negative way say, 'Yeah, I tried a counsellor, but I didn't like them so I didn't go back'—as with any service, keep trying until you get a good one.

Another complaint about counselling is that a couple of sessions failed to make any difference—it's like going to the gym, you don't go once or twice then expect to be buff. If you want to make a change in your life, it often takes some dedication.

Due to long waiting lists, people often make a counselling appointment and by the time it comes around, they've moved on from that particular issue. I reckon you should still go and discuss what happened, how you got through it, and how you helped yourself. There's nothing wrong with rocking up to a counselling appointment feeling happy—it's important to notice feeling happy too!

Whose side are you on?

Most importantly, if stuff is a bit tricky, be nice to yourself. There're plenty of people who will give you a hard time—why help them out?

TRICKY QUESTIONS

Q How can I stop being violent?

A Big question—first off, if you're asking this question you're well on the way. Lots of people don't think about the violence in their lives because they don't even recognise it as violence—it's just 'stuff that happens'. Why bother trying to change if you think nothing's wrong?

Violence impacts not only on your health, your sense of safety and wellbeing, but on those around you too—your loved ones. Violence destroys relationships.

Getting informed is essential. There are plenty of people around who are more than happy to support people to end the cycle of violence. Domestic violence services, and health and youth centres are all good starting points.

Body awareness is a useful tool for discovering your triggers (what sets you off) and your warning signs (signs that you're getting stressed—feeling flushed, slow breathing, headache, etc.). Avoiding your triggers as much as possible and developing coping skills that don't involve violence are all a part of creating a life without violence.

It can be important to find ways of feeling powerful in a relationship that don't involve violence or power tactics. This takes time and dedication—how do people feel powerful in a relationship without taking power away from their partner? Breaking the cycle of violence is challenging, but living a life without the constant pressure or threat of violence is definitely worth it.

Q My medication has stopped me cumming. How can I bring up pleasure with my doctor?

A Doctors are starting to realise that people's sexual functioning is equally, if not more, important to them than their mental health. I've heard of many people stopping their medication to regain their ability to enjoy sex. Raising pleasure in relation to health and wellbeing is a good way to discuss your needs with your doctor as pleasure and sexual expression is good for your overall health.

One thing that's useful to remember is that your doctor is there for you. If you don't feel like you're getting good health care from your doctor, try and find one who will provide the level of care you're looking for. There are many different medications on the market—some have greater impacts on sex and sexuality than others, and your doctor may be able to support you to find the right one for you. It's important to consult with your doctor before changing any of your medications.

Q My partner is thinking of having an abortion. How can I support her?

A Ask your partner how you can support her. It's important to discuss your views on abortion, but it's really important to realise that it's her body that's going on the line so she gets to make the final decision. It can be really hard if you want to go ahead with the pregnancy. Just keep in mind that women don't make these decisions lightly—it is often really scary for her too, so your support is essential. She might want you to go along for any appointments or on the day of the abortion. She might want to take a friend instead or go on her own. She might want to talk about it or she might want to forget all about it. She might want you around or she might want some space. Keep the lines of communication open so you keep in touch with what's going on for each other. Chances are you'll both be needing a bit of support. How you show your care and concern at tricky times like this can really strengthen a relationship.

Don't forget to talk your stuff out too. Finding your own support might benefit you as well as your partner.

Feelings of relief, sadness, guilt and wondering about the decision are all common. Couples often feel more relief and less sadness over time but, as with any grief and loss issue, people can get stuck. If sleeping and eating patterns change dramatically, it can be a sign that extra support is needed. There can be subtle pressure for couples to 'get over it'. That's not only harsh but unrealistic. These are major life decisions that can have long-reaching implications. Many services that provide abortions also provide extensive, ongoing counselling.

Chapter 8

The Future

'The future? I dunno, look after yourself now—wrap it up [wear a condom] so you *have* a future.'

'You might not be enjoying your relationship right now, but you can start planning your future relationships. How do you want it to be? It's up to you.'

Looking after your health, looking after your fertility

Looking after your health is a lifelong gig. There's a saying, 'I'm not here for a long time, I'm here for a good time'—stuff that, I reckon I'm here for a long, good time. The majority of sexual health dramas that can happen to guys are related to lifestyle factors—how we live our life can affect our sex.

Having kids might not be a big deal to you at the moment, but later down the track you may think differently. Looking after your fertility now may prevent heartache and costly procedures later on.

Fertility facts for men

Sperm quality and quantity start to drop from age 35, and is related to lifestyle. Poor lifestyle choices include drugs, alcohol, smoking and weight gain. These can have the following effects:

- reduced fertility
- decreased sperm quality
- increased miscarriage rates
- increased birth abnormalities
- children's health affected.

Added to this is the fact that some STIs can lead to infertility if left untreated. So how can you protect your fertility?

SAFER SEX

Always practising safer sex can prevent STIs. Regular sexual health checks can make sure that any STIs are quickly spotted.

GOOD HEALTH

Some people say good health is the sexiest thing someone can wear. A healthy balanced diet is a good start, along with regular exercise. Looking after your body is not only good for you in general, it's good for your sex life and maintaining your fertility—and while it's good for you now, it also sets you up to be healthier in the future.

EVEN MORE REASON NOT TO SMOKE

Not only can smoking affect your erections, it changes the shape of your sperm, affecting the way they swim. If that's not enough, smoking smells really bad.

Marijuana affects blood pressure and sperm development in much the same way.

If you'd like support to stop smoking, go to www.quitsa.org.au or contact the Cancer Council in your state.

UNDERWEAR

Some people suggest that wearing cotton boxers instead of briefs can keep the testicles cooler, reducing heat stress, but studies have provided mixed results. However, avoiding major heat on your testicles is a good tip; that's why they're in the scrotum, outside of the abdomen—they're air-cooled.

LOOK AFTER YOUR BALLS

Wear protective gear if you're playing sports where there's a possibility of damaging your testicles. If you get a whack, get your doctor to check them out.

Sometimes our testicles can get twisted. It's very important to get medical treatment as soon as possible—their blood supply could possibly be cut off and you could end up losing a testicle or two.

If you're about to start a course of medicine or therapy (e.g. chemotherapy) that could affect your fertility, you might want to store some sperm. Your doctor will be able to refer you to a reproductive clinic that will give you more info on sperm storage.

'HOW WELL DO I LOOK AFTER MYSELF?'

Learner for life

Okay, you've read this book, but where to now? Well, apart from the practical side of things (actually doing it), there's so much information out there that you could spend your life studying sex and sexuality. There're literally thousands of years of sexuality to explore.

You might want to explore your own cultural or religious attitudes to sex and sexuality through history. Or, you might just want to learn more about sex. Search your library or use the internet to find out more. Here are a few teachings to get you started:

» *Kama Sutra*—Make sure you get the version with the commentary that explains what's going on.
» *Ananga Ranga*—Another text created to spice up your sex life.
» *Tao Te Ching*—Part of this book focuses on the Tao of sex. Taoists believe good sex can cure many health complaints.
» Tantric sex—'Tantra' literally means expanding, so tantric sex looks at expanding our understanding and experience of sex.

The choices you make now can affect you later on in life. It's good to have some goals about how you want to live your life. Think about the following:

» What kind of guy do you want to be ?
» What kind of relationships do you want to have?
» Do you want to have a long and happy sex life ?
» How will you treat your partner?
» How will you expect to be treated?
» What kind of sexual reputation do you want to have? This can be especially important if you live in a small town where everyone knows everyone else.
» What kind of messages do you want to pass on to your kids? Do you want them to feel shame, fear and guilt or do you want them to enjoy the sex they have?
» How will you make sure you have sex without regret?

TRICKY QUESTIONS

Q What should I have in my emergency sexual health toolkit?

A Sexual health toolkit practical essential:

- condoms lots and lots of them
- lube—water-based
- gloves
- dams
- if you've got a female partner on the pill—a spare pack of her pills just in case she forgets her own
- perhaps a back-up supply of emergency contraception
- contact numbers for your nearest sexual health clinic
- *Kama Sutra* of course!
- an open mind
- a sense of humour
- a sex-positive attitude
- pride
- bravery
- honesty
- care and compassion

LAST WORD

I thought I'd leave the last word for one of the guys I'd interviewed:

**'Sex is such a healthy, healing thing—
what a great way to celebrate being alive.'**

Learning More

SOME COOL BOOKS TO READ

Dick: A guide to the penis for men and women by Caroline de Costa and Michele Moore. Allen & Unwin, Crows Nest, 2003

'It Happened to Me': A teen's guide to overcoming sexual abuse, by William Lee Carter. New Harbinger Publications, 2002

Puberty Boy by Geoff Price. Allen & Unwin, Crows Nest, 2005

Riding the Sexual Frontier: All you ever wanted to know about men and sex by Jo-Anne Baker. Harper Collins Publishers, 2002

Satisfaction: The art of the female orgasm by Kim Cattrall and Mark Levinson. Thorsons, an imprint of Harper Collins Publishers, 2002

Sex Tips: Advice from women experts from around the world by Jo-Anne Baker. Allen & Unwin, Crows Nest, 1999

Tantric Sex: Making love last by Cassandra Lorius. Thorsons, an imprint of Harper Collins Publishers, 1999

Urge by Dr Gabrielle Morrissey. Harper Collins Publishers, 2002

The V Book: Vital facts about the vulva, vestibule, vagina and more by Dr Elizabeth Stewart and Paula Spencer. Piatkus Publishers, 2002

SOME COOL WEBSITES TO VISIT

The internet can have lots of really useful information, but don't believe everything you read—there are some dodgy sites out there. Here're some that I've found to be useful . . .

Abortion/termination

www.menandabortion.com
This is a site specifically for men about abortion. Guys are often left out of conversations about abortion. This site has lots of useful information for guys whose partner is contemplating or has already had an abortion. Great FAQs, resources and real-life stories.

Body image

www.adiosbarbie.com
The mission of 'Adiós, Barbie' is to promote a healthy self and body image for folks of all races, cultures and sizes. Great articles, humour, research and ad/myth busting.

www.completelygorgeous.com.au
Kaz Cooke's site looks at a range of body image issues—there's even a section on penis size. Lots of body image information is targeted at women but there's a lot of evidence that guys are also affected by body image.

Fertility

www.thinkfertility.com.au
Having a baby might not be that important to you right now, but it can be a good idea to look after your fertility (your ability to have a baby) so you can make the choice later in life. This site has lots of useful information for men, women and couples wanting to learn more about planning a pregnancy and protecting their fertility.

HIV/AIDS

www.afao.org.au
Every state in Australia has an AIDS Council but the Australian Federation of AIDS Organisations (AFAO) is the peak organisation. You can get local links via this website but it also has great information about HIV prevention, laws and living well with HIV.

Intersex and transgender issues

www.isna.org
The Intersex Society of North America (ISNA) site has lots of information and links to support individuals and their families. ISNA is devoted to changing the way people who are born with genitals who aren't clearly male or female are handled by the medical community and society in general.

www.gendercentre.org.au
The Gender Centre in Sydney provides services for people with gender issues, but also has a great range of resources including fact sheets and *Polare* magazine—great reading for anyone interested in finding more about 'trans' issues.

Law information

www.lawstuff.org.au
National Children's and Youth Law Centre provides lots of advice and information about your legal rights and responsibilities, and not just about sex.

Men's health

www.xyonline.net
This site is full on. There are lots of opportunities to get involved with women-positive men and find out what other guys are doing to make our community safer for everyone.

www.andrologyaustralia.org
This site is a community and professional education program. They provide quality information about male reproductive health.

Mental health

www.headroom.net.au
'Headroom' is a positive mental health site, and provides lots of info for young people by young people looking at issues like stress, peer pressure, bullying, conflict, optimism and relationships. Check out their pamphlets—they've got everything!

www.reachout.com.au
'Reachout' is a space to explore issues that are important to your mental health and wellbeing. This site provides info, support and skills development aimed at young people.

www.moodgym.anu.edu.au
A free self-help program to teach cognitive behaviour therapy skills to people vulnerable to depression and anxiety.

Relationship or domestic violence

Warning: if you are in a violent relationship these sites may be used against you by a partner checking your internet history. If you think this might be a possibility you can access these sites via a friend's computer or the local library, health or youth centre.

www.endabuse.org
This site is run by the Family Violence Prevention Fund and aims to promote a world free from violence. A great site to help you understand violence and make a stand against it.

www.dontcrosstheline.com.au
A great Australian site for guys that provides a range of strategies for stopping violence.

www.burstingthebubble.com
Another great site about family violence—what it is and how to stop it.

Same-sex attraction

There is a range of services for young people exploring their sexuality. These ones are based in South Australia, but they will be able to provide you with info about services closer to you.

www.insideout.cyh.com
'InSide Out' is a service for young men who are attracted to other guys. Their website has a range of useful information on topics from coming out to safety.

www.ucwesleyadelaide.org.au/bfriend
'Bfriend' is a program that provides support for people of all ages who are wondering about their sexuality/gender identity and/or people who are just starting to identify as same-sex attracted/gay/lesbian/bisexual/transgender/intersex or queer. There are heaps of useful stories and links.

www.rainbowfamilytree.com
A very interactive site where queer digital storytellers and their friends and families can upload their own digital story and view other people's.

Sexual health

www.shinesa.org.au
This is where I work, so you might even see a picture of me looking professional! There're interesting facts about sexually transmissible infections, contraception, pregnancy, etc.

www.likeitis.org.au
This site has lots of interactive games, lots of questions and answers and they use some super role models and ambassadors to spread the word of positive sexual health . . . and make sure you play their 'Cool or fool' game.

www.yoursexhealth.org
One of the coolest sites around with heaps of info about reproduction, how you live your life, female matters, male matters, sexual practices, sexual safety and communication—great info and great visuals (in my opinion).

www.thehormonefactory.com
Another great site—check out the 'What do you think?' section, which lets you have your say about a range of sex health topics.

Sexually transmissible infections (STIs)

www.stdservices.on.net
A no-messing-about site run by Clinic 275—just the facts about STIs—what are they, how do they get transmitted, what are the symptoms, how are they treated and how you can protect yourself.

Sexual violence

www.yarrowplace.sa.gov.au
'Yarrow Place' is a service that provides counselling, support and information for people who have been raped or sexually assaulted, as well as providing information for the community to better understand rape and sexual assault.

Tantric sex

www.tantra.com
This site has plenty of information to expand your understandings of sex and sexuality, but be warned there are some explicit images on this site and there are some adverts on here too. Beware of people exploiting your curiosity of sex.

Youth issues

www.cyh.com
This site has everything you need to know for a healthy body, mind and relationship.

www.somazone.com.au
This site provides fast, free, anonymous access to health information—and you can share some of your stuff. Check out the 'Tell your story' section.

www.goaskalice.columbia.edu
This site is run by Columbia University and has a heap of health information—everything from fitness and nutrition to emotional health, giving up smoking and sexuality. You can even send in your own questions—Go ask Alice!

WHERE I FOUND MY INFORMATION

'Australian study of health and relationships' by La Trobe University; Central Sydney Area Health Service; and the national centres in HIV Social Research and HIV Epidemiology and Clinical Research, University of NSW, 2002

'Men and sex and fear and intimacy' by Norman Dean Radican, *On the Level*, vol. 3, no. 4

Sexual Behaviour in the Human Male by A. Kinsey. Indiana University Press, Bloomington, USA, 1975

'Sexual factors and prostate cancer' by Graeme Giles et al., *British Journal of Urology*, vol. 92, pp. 211–16

Urge by Dr Gabrielle Morrissey. Harper Collins Publishers, 2002

Writing Themselves in Again: 6 years on: pp. 36–8, *The 2nd national report on the sexuality, health and well-being of same sex attracted young people in Australia* by Lynne Hillier, Anne Mitchell and Alina Turner. Australian Research Centre in Sex, Health and Society (ARCSHS), La Trobe University Melbourne, 2005

http://www3.interscience.wiley.com/cgi-bin/fulltext/118853726/PDFSTART